W9-BYY-285

easy KETO MEAL PREP

4 weeks of healthy ketogenic meal plans with 100+ simple recipes for any day of the week

JENNY CASTANEDA

VICTORY BELT PUBLISHING INC.

Las Vegas

First published in 2019 by Victory Belt Publishing Inc.

Copyright © 2019 Jenny Castaneda

All rights reserved

No part of this publication may be reproduced or distributed in any form or by any means, electronic or mechanical, or stored in a database or retrieval system, without prior written permission from the publisher.

ISBN-13: 978-1-628603-86-6

The author is not a licensed practitioner, physician, or medical professional and offers no medical diagnoses, treatments, suggestions, or counseling. The information presented herein has not been evaluated by the U.S. Food and Drug Administration, and it is not intended to diagnose, treat, cure, or prevent any disease. Full medical clearance from a licensed physician should be obtained before beginning or modifying any diet, exercise, or lifestyle program, and physicians should be informed of all nutritional changes.

The author claims no responsibility to any person or entity for any liability, loss, or damage caused or alleged to be caused directly or indirectly as a result of the use, application, or interpretation of the information presented herein.

Front and back cover photography by Will Wohlgezogen and Jenny Castaneda

Lifestyle photos by Priscilla Caraveo Photography

Cover design by Justin-Aaron Velasco

Interior design and illustrations by Kat Lannom, Crizalie Olimpo, Eli San Juan, and Allan Santos

Printed in Canada
TC 0119

TABLE OF CONTENTS

Part 1: *introduction*

WHY I WROTE THIS BOOK

Imagine not having to figure out what to eat, turn on the stove, cook, and then clean up every single night. Instead, you open your refrigerator and are greeted with the most beautiful sight ever: containers filled with ready-to-eat healthy keto meals stacked on top of each other. High-five for #fridgegoals! You heat up anything you want to eat, and in less than five minutes you're fueling your body with delicious food while hanging out with the family or catching up on your favorite shows. No stress, no mess, no precious time wasted. *Sounds amazing, doesn't it?*

Do you think this is too good to be true? What if I tell you that this can be you if you incorporate meal prepping into your weekly routine? Meal prepping will help you work smarter, not harder, by using time efficiently so you can focus on other important things throughout the week without derailing your healthy eating habits.

Enter *Easy Keto Meal Prep*. This comprehensive four-week meal prep guide provides you with an easy-to-follow game plan that will help you stock your refrigerator with nutrient-dense and tasty meals that you and your family can enjoy for a whole week.

The recipes in this book use simple ingredients that are readily available at any grocery store. Designate one day a week as your dedicated meal-prep day (or pick two days if that's more convenient for you). On those days, you cook six or seven meals that you can mix and match. This means you aren't eating the same thing for five straight days! (Because "I want to eat the same meal the entire week," said no one ever.)

Easy Keto Meal Prep contains four "done-for-you" plans, so you don't have to think about what to eat, create a grocery list, or plan your prep and cook days. Following these four plans will help you get into the habit of preparing your meals weekly so you have enough food for breakfast, lunch, and dinner. The plans also include free meal days so you can still enjoy a meal out or plan for social events.

Whether you're a keto newbie or a seasoned pro, I've put together resources to help you succeed every week by making the recipes and plans super easy to understand and use. This makes sticking to your keto lifestyle more sustainable and enjoyable!

I started meal prepping at the end of 2015 when my friends Diane Sanfilippo and Tony Kasandrinos and I decided to incorporate counting macros into our lifting and workout routines. Counting macros was tough, but prepping the majority of my meals ahead of time was fun. Before I knew it, I was doing it consistently on Sundays every week. It never felt like work because I really enjoyed cooking and preparing the food.

I shared my weekly videos on Snapchat and then transitioned to Instagram because I wanted to be able to share them with more people. Soon, I released my Four-Week Meal Prep Challenges, which were downloadable PDFs. They contained meal plans, grocery lists, and a game plan to follow. I had a private group of participants on Facebook who showed up each week for accountability and posted updates and photos about the meals they'd cooked by following the plans and recipes in the challenge. Everyone had a lot of fun and shared insight and feedback with fellow meal preppers.

In mid-2018, I decided to give keto a try, so I shifted the focus of my weekly meal prep videos on Instagram to keto meals. I wanted to continue my Four-Week Meal Prep Challenges, but I wondered, "What if I turn it into a really good book resource and beef it up with all the information that I regularly share online?" I got to work and experimented with recipes, developed meal plans with complementary flavors, and created detailed game plans that I knew would make meal prepping easy to do. I came up with a deep-dive guide that explains the purpose of each section of the done-for-you plans.

If you came across this book because you're interested in keto or meal prepping (or both!), I'd like to invite you to head over to my Instagram (@cookandsavor) to follow along with my Sunday weekly meal preps. Feel free to drop me a quick DM or comment on my latest post to say, "Hey!" and ask me any questions you have. I love one-on-one conversations, so don't be shy! If we're already connected on Instagram and you're familiar with the recipes, videos, tips, and tricks that I've regularly been sharing there, I'm sure you'll also enjoy cooking with *Easy Keto Meal Prep*!

MEAL PREP 411

Meal prepping is taking the time to cook the majority of your meals for the week ahead of time. Gone are the days of last-minute decisions about what to eat or feed the family for breakfast, lunch, or dinner because meal prepping puts nutrient-dense, ready-to-eat meals within arm's reach.

Meal prepping not only saves you money but also allows you to spend more time with your family. And the chances that you'll make unhealthy food choices will be slim to none!

I know you've been in a situation where you're on your way home from work or school, exhausted and so hungry, with no clue what to eat for dinner. Your body wants to be fed, so you detour to the nearest fast-food joint to grab something because you MUST. EAT. NOW.

Let's change that situation, shall we? What if you know that there's food ready to be eaten as soon as you get home? You're tired and hungry, yes, but you're not in a panic trying to figure out what to eat; rather, you're mentally picturing the inside of your refrigerator, trying to decide which home-cooked meal you will heat up and eat in less than five minutes. Because you know this, you find it easier to drive past that fast-food joint on your way home.

Why Is Meal Prepping Important?

Here are the top three reasons why meal prepping is important:

- It saves time.

- It saves money.

- It leaves less opportunity for you to make unhealthy food choices.

There's just something about opening a fridge full of food that instantly makes you happy!

Other meal preppers have told me that they like meal prepping because they can spend more time with the family on weeknights and because they have more time to relax and decompress at the end of the day.

"But Jenny," you might say, "meal prepping takes a lot of time and work!"

Why yes, yes it does. Unless you have a budget to buy ready-to-eat meals made with good-quality ingredients, such as the meals from Balanced Bites (and no, frozen TV dinners do not count!), or to hire someone to cook for you, you need to put in the work at the start of the week so you can reap the benefits of your efforts in the following days. Meal prepping requires an investment of time, but it's time well spent. If you calculate the number of hours you cook each night to prepare that night's dinner and meals for the following day, the total will be significantly more than the time you will spend during once-a-week or twice-a-week meal prep sessions.

My husband, Will, and I both work our regular jobs, all day, Monday to Friday. He gets home around 4:00 p.m. I get home even later—closer to 6:00 p.m. By the time I walk in the door, we're both hungry, but we're not stressed about what to eat because we prepped our meals the Sunday before. We take a minute or two to decide what's for dinner, heat up our plates, and then it's chow time. These premade meals are a *huge* help on the weeks Will's son, Diego, is with us. He's usually hungry when Will picks him up after school. Instead of grabbing the usual burger and fries from In-N-Out or pizza from Pizza Hut to eat when he gets home, Will gives Diego a more nutritious snack, such as a chicken drumstick or pork chop with cut-up vegetables, to tide him over until dinnertime. Diego doesn't eat keto, so I have a few of his simple go-to meals prepped and ready for him.

Not only does our family eat well but we also save money each month because we prepare 90 percent of our meals at home, but we still enjoy a meal out once a week. As you get into meal prepping, you may notice that you'll spend a little more on groceries than you did before, but you don't need to worry. The amount you spend as you meal prep still will be significantly less than what you'd spend on the combination of groceries, fast food, and eating out multiple times each week. For our family of two adults and one child, our weekly grocery bill is around $150. We do most of our shopping at Trader Joe's and grab one or two specialty items at Whole Foods. Eating ethically sourced, humanely raised meat from grass-fed and pasture-raised animals is very important to us, so we also subscribe to a monthly meat delivery box from Moink for $159. Our grocery bill comes out to $759 a month for three meals a day plus snacks for six or seven days a week. Breaking this down even more, that amounts to $25 each day and $8 per meal.

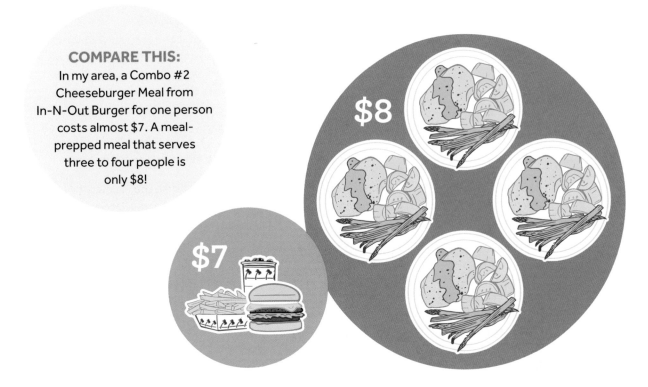

COMPARE THIS:
In my area, a Combo #2 Cheeseburger Meal from In-N-Out Burger for one person costs almost $7. A meal-prepped meal that serves three to four people is only $8!

$8

$7

When Should You Meal Prep?

Now that I've convinced you that meal prepping will be beneficial, you may be wondering when is the most appropriate time to get it done. There's no set day to meal prep; it depends on your home or work schedule and when you can most easily carve out some time. The majority of people (including me) meal prep on the weekend, usually on a Sunday, so the food is good through the rest of the work or school week. If you have different "weekends" or work shifts, pick the day that's most convenient for you.

If you're just starting, you may want to split the work between two days by including a midweek meal prep day, such as Wednesday. That way, you're not cooking as much in a single day, which can make it feel like a chore. For each of the four weekly done-for-you plans, I've included two approaches: Cook Once a Week and Cook Twice a Week. As you get more comfortable with meal prepping, you can switch from two meal prep days to just one. On the other hand, if you typically cook once a week but find yourself with a shorter-than-usual time window to do your meal prep for the week ahead, you can switch to twice a week. I've made the plans flexible enough for you to choose what works best for you.

If you're more experienced and you want free rein on which entrée and side dish to combine to create a meal for yourself and your family each day, you can download a blank template from **easyketomealprep.com** and create a DIY plan using the recipes included with each week.

Meal Planning vs. Meal Prepping

The terms meal planning and meal prepping sometimes are used interchangeably, which can get confusing because the two things seem the same, but they're not. Meal planning is the precursor to meal prepping; it's the process of determining which recipes to cook for which meals and then coming up with a grocery list before you head to the store. After this phase comes the execution part, which is meal prepping. Cutting, chopping, sautéing, baking, and stir-frying meals one after the other, or sometimes at the same time, happens as a result of good meal planning.

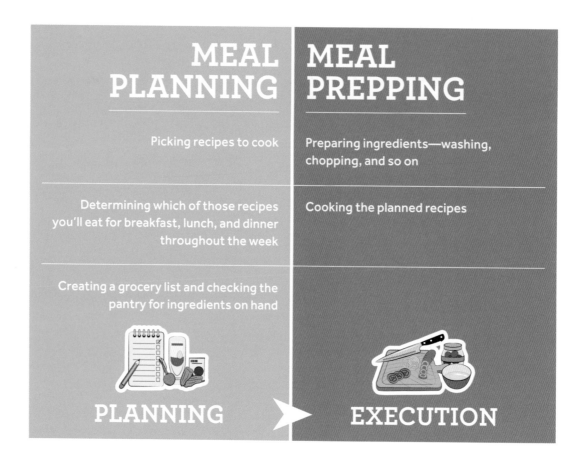

MEAL PLANNING	MEAL PREPPING
Picking recipes to cook	Preparing ingredients—washing, chopping, and so on
Determining which of those recipes you'll eat for breakfast, lunch, and dinner throughout the week	Cooking the planned recipes
Creating a grocery list and checking the pantry for ingredients on hand	
PLANNING	EXECUTION

If you're no stranger to meal planning, you know it can take some time depending on how many recipes you plan to cook. Sometimes you'll get stuck in a rut trying to come up with ideas while browsing online and even while going through your tried-and-true recipes, which leaves you feeling frustrated because nothing is jumping out at you. When my brother and I were kids, my mom would always ask us on Saturday mornings before she went to the market what dishes we wanted to eat during the week, and we'd both give her that deer-in-the-headlights look because we couldn't think of anything. Thankfully, my mom is pretty savvy, so she'd always come up with yummy meals for us after going through her recipe notebook and checking out what was on sale. Meal planning can be time-consuming, but it's worth the effort because doing it right will help you be able to meal prep successfully.

Fear not; I've done four weeks' worth of meal planning for you, so you don't have to worry about anything. Review each week's meal plan, shop for groceries, and then get your meal prep on!

BUILDING A KETO PLATE

Easy Keto Meal Prep does not dive deep into the details of what keto is all about because there are so many books already available. This book is designed to simplify the keto diet and make it more sustainable for you to follow by providing weekly meal plans that follow a ketogenic template. If you want to read more about keto, I recommend checking out a couple of books in the "Recommended Products, Brands, and Resources" section (page 304).

In a nutshell, the ketogenic, or keto, diet involves consuming high amounts of fat, moderate amounts of protein, and low amounts of carbohydrates. This division of nutrients enables your body to burn fat as fuel rather than burning carbohydrates and sugar as you would if you followed other types of diets. When you are burning fat for fuel, you are said to be "in ketosis."

Do you find yourself trying to figure out how to build a keto plate without meticulously counting or weighing your food? Follow this three-step approach, which has worked really well for me:

1. Start with 3 to 5 ounces of fatty protein (a palm-sized portion).

2. Add one serving of low-carb vegetables (2 cups light leafy greens or 1 cup cooked veggies).

3. Add one serving of fat (about 1 tablespoon).

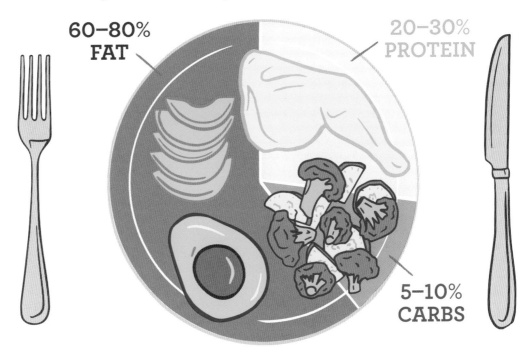

If you still feel hungry after eating a meal, your body is signaling you that it needs a little more fat. Add an extra serving of fat when necessary, and you'll notice that you feel satisfied. Once your body has adapted to getting the majority of its calories from fat, there will be times when you'll feel like you don't need to eat as much food, so adjust your intake accordingly. Don't think that you need to eat specific quantities at every meal. Keep modifying to figure out what works best for you!

MEAL PREPPING WHILE EATING A KETO DIET

What Is "Keto Flu"?

Transitioning your body into a fat-burning machine when it always has been fueled by carbohydrates takes a little bit of time. You will feel lethargic, fuzzy, and irritable at first, and you might even get headaches, as if your body is fighting off a bug. However, these symptoms mean you're not getting enough electrolytes, such as sodium. To help remedy this shortfall, hydrate with a pitcher of refreshing Citrus Electrolyte Drink (page 298) until you're feeling normal again.

If you're currently eating keto, you may be used to drinking your breakfast in the form of a hearty cup of butter coffee (and that's okay if that works for you), but you won't find butter coffee in any of the weekly meal plans in Easy Keto Meal Prep. *I want you to be able to sit down, chew your food, enjoy it, and appreciate the feeling of satiety you get from polishing off a filling breakfast.*

I loved the way I felt once my body was in ketosis and burning fat, but boy, was it a rough couple of weeks when I first started! Headaches, brain fog, and fatigue were my top three keto flu symptoms, so I made sure I hydrated my body well with water and added an extra teaspoon of Himalayan sea salt daily to replenish electrolytes. Suddenly, I woke up one day feeling bright-eyed and bushy-tailed! I knew then that my body had adapted, and it was all smooth sailing from there. After a month of eating keto, I no longer had food cravings, and I didn't feel intense hunger (like I was going to pass out if I didn't eat), which meant that my blood sugar levels were super stable. It was amazing!

I must say, my weekly meal prepping helped make my transition to eating keto much easier than it might have been. I continued to prepare proteins and vegetables but used fattier cuts of meat and added more healthy fats to each meal. I cut down on prepping carbohydrates because my usual rice, potatoes, and purple sweet potatoes were no longer part of my meals. I did miss carbs at first (especially rice), but once my body was in ketosis, I no longer wanted any of it. Now, I keep my daily carbohydrates between 25 and 30 grams and eat as much fat and protein as I want.

Eating keto doesn't mean overindulging in meat, cheese, and fats. Every meal in this book has a good balance of healthy fats, protein, and a generous serving of vegetables. I have friends who poo-pooed keto because they gained weight, hated it, or found that it caused them health issues after giving it a try. Apparently they were eating an unbalanced diet and were trying to live on bacon and butter coffee! I know you've heard this before, but eating balanced meals is very important, no matter what diet you're following.

Eating vegetables to get enough fiber is necessary because it helps keep you full longer and makes your digestive system happy; also, vegetables provide micronutrients that your body needs. Add a serving of leafy greens to your plate so you always have a nutritionally complete meal. These types of greens are very low in carbohydrates, so you don't need to worry about going over your daily carbohydrate limit!

STAPLE INGREDIENTS FOR EASY KETO MEAL PREPPING

There are a lot of keto-friendly ingredients out there, but this section focuses on those that are staples for meal prepping and that you'll use in recipes throughout this book. This list will come in handy when you are trying to keto-fy a favorite recipe or when you're planning a meal from scratch.

What's the Deal with Net Carbs?

Net carbs are carbohydrates such as starch and sugar that have a significant impact on the body's blood sugar level. They are broken down into glucose (sugar) that the body uses for energy.

Fiber, which is a carbohydrate but can't be digested easily, doesn't factor into net carbs. Sugar alcohol such as Swerve (erythritol), which you'll find in some of the dessert recipes in this book, also doesn't count toward net carbs. Sugar alcohols are derived from plants and have a similar sweetness to regular sugar, but they don't affect blood sugar levels.

Here's how you calculate net carbs:

Net Carbs = Total Carbs – Fiber – Sugar Alcohol (if used)

The nutritional information for each recipe displays the net carbs rather than the total carbs, so you won't need to calculate the net carbs.

FATTY PROTEIN	SERVING SIZE	MACROS		
		FAT	PROTEIN	NET CARBS
Beef, ground (80/20)	4 ounces	22g	19g	0g
Beef, rib-eye	4 ounces	22g	28g	0g
Beef, chuck roast	4 ounces	17g	28g	0g
Eggs	1 large	5g	6g	0g
Pork, ground	4 ounces	24g	29g	0g
Pork chop, boneless	4 ounces	17g	30g	0g
Pork butt or shoulder	4 ounces	21g	27g	0g
Pork, sausage	2 links	13g	9g	1g
Bacon	3 slices	12g	12g	0g
Chicken thigh, boneless, skinless	1 thigh	18g	31g	0g
Turkey, ground dark meat	4 ounces	20g	28g	0g
Wild salmon	4 ounces	14g	25g	0g

HEALTHY FATS	SERVING SIZE	MACROS		
		FAT	PROTEIN	NET CARBS
Avocado, Hass	1 small	22g	3g	3g
Avocado oil	1 tablespoon	14g	0g	0g
Butter	1 tablespoon	12g	0g	0g
Coconut butter	1 tablespoon	14g	0g	0g
Coconut milk	⅓ cup	19g	2g	2g
Coconut oil	1 tablespoon	14g	0g	0g
Ghee	1 tablespoon	12.7g	0g	0g
Olive oil	1 tablespoon	14g	0g	0g
Olives	10 olives	11g	1g	3g
Cheese (goat, sheep, or cow)	1 ounce	8g	6g	0g
Heavy cream	1 ounce	11g	1g	1g
Almonds	¼ cup	11g	5g	2g
Macadamia nuts	¼ cup	21g	2g	1.5g
Peanuts	¼ cup	14g	7g	2g
Pecans	¼ cup	20g	2.5g	1g
Walnuts	¼ cup	18g	4g	2g
Tahini	1 tablespoon	8g	3g	3g

LOW-CARB PRODUCE AND HERBS	SERVING SIZE	MACROS		
		FAT	PROTEIN	NET CARBS
Asparagus	5 spears	0g	2g	1.5g
Baby arugula	1 cup	0g	0g	0g
Baby bok choy	1 cup	0g	2g	3g
Basil	⅓ cup	0g	0g	0g
Bell peppers	½ cup	0g	0.5g	3g
Broccoli	1 cup	0g	2.5g	3.5g
Cabbage	1 cup	0g	1g	3g
Cauliflower	1 cup	0g	2g	3g
Cilantro	¼ cup	0g	0g	0g
Cucumber	1 cup	0g	1g	6g
Garlic	1 clove	0g	0g	0g
Ginger	1 teaspoon	0g	0g	0g
Green beans	1 cup	0g	2g	4g
Green onions	¼ cup	0g	0g	1g
Jalapeño peppers	1 pepper	0g	0g	0g
Kale	1 cup	0g	1g	1g
Lemon	1 fruit	0g	1g	5g
Lime	1 fruit	0g	1g	5g
Mushrooms	½ cup	1g	3g	5g
Parsley	¼ cup	0g	0g	0g
Snow peas	1 cup	0g	5g	6g
Spaghetti squash	1 cup	0g	1g	7g
Spinach	1 cup	0g	1g	0.5g
Swiss chard	1 cup	0g	3g	4g
Tomato	½ cup	0g	1g	2g
Yellow squash	1 cup	1g	2g	5g
Zucchini	1 cup	1g	3g	4g

TIPS AND TRICKS

I believe that with the right mind-set and tools, you're capable of nailing every meal prep session, even if you feel a little overwhelmed and unsure at first. Here are my top five tips and tricks, which you can refer to again and again when you need a little bit of guidance.

KISS—Keep It Super Simple

What helped me a lot at first was starting with simple recipes and dishes that were already part of my regular rotation. You don't need to cook gourmet meals with a dozen ingredients and steps. Save those for a special occasion; for everyday cooking, pick recipes that are quick and easy without a lot of fuss.

Whether you're a novice or an advanced meal prepper, you should incorporate basic recipes that you can easily mix and match. Think baked chicken breasts, grilled flank steak, steamed cauliflower rice, and blanched or roasted veggies. A couple of these are always on my menu because they require minimal prep work and are fairly easy to cook.

Remember that preparing basic recipes cuts down on the total amount of time you spend cooking; plus, you can jazz them up to create different meals in just a few minutes.

Using meal prep shortcuts cuts down prep time significantly. I give you shortcut suggestions in each week's meal plan to give you an idea of how you can save even more time.

Make Time for Meal Prepping

I can't stress this point enough. Not having enough time to meal prep is the number-one reason I hear people say they can't do it. Setting aside a few hours per week by marking it on your calendar helps a lot. You make time to do laundry, tidy up the house, shower, and get the kids ready for school. You *can* make time to meal prep, too. "I'm too busy" should never be an excuse. If eating healthy and having ready-to-eat meals are important to you, you can make time to meal prep.

Once meal prepping has become a part of your routine, you won't even have to think twice about doing it!

Make the Work Fun

Yes, meal prepping *is* work, but that doesn't mean you have to treat it as such. One way to make meal prep feel less like work is by listening to your favorite jams so you can sing along and dance as you cook. You'll find that music helps the time pass really quickly, and you'll be done before you know it.

Every Sunday, my dad would play songs from Neil Diamond, John Denver, the Beatles, and the Stylistics—to name a few—when we were all hanging out at home doing chores. These tunes bring back wonderful memories that always make me smile. So I put together a playlist of this music (you can find it on my blog), and I often listen to it when I meal prep because it reminds me of my childhood and those songs my family listened to when I was growing up.

Many Hands Make Light Work

If you have a significant other or kids who are old enough to help in the kitchen, encourage them to give you a hand. Explain why you're meal prepping and the importance of having ready-made meals during the week (for example, so that you have more time to relax and fewer dishes to clean) to help them understand the purpose of helping out.

Will is my designated sous chef on meal prep days. He's responsible for vegetable and other ingredient prep as well as kitchen cleanup. This arrangement works out well because, as much as I love cooking, cleaning up is my least favorite chore!

Cook Several Meals at the Same Time

I always plan my menu to take full advantage of the stove, oven, and sometimes the Instant Pot. There's no need for fancy gadgets; a basic oven range is more than enough. You can cook two meals on the stove simultaneously; for example, you can have a sauce simmering low and slow while you're pan-searing some meat. A tray of vegetables and a sheet-pan dinner can go in the oven together, so that's four items cooking at the same time!

You'll make the majority of the meals in this book with the stove and oven, and your weekly Meal Prep Game Plan guides you through the order for cooking meals.

WHAT'S YOUR EXCUSE?

You know by now that I'm passionate about meal prepping. Every time I get a chance to talk about it to family and friends (or random strangers, such as the cashier at Trader Joe's), more often than not I get an excuse for why the person doesn't meal prep or won't even consider giving it a try. The number-one excuse? Food boredom.

Food Boredom

People tell me that they don't like to meal prep because they easily get bored with eating the same plain meal over and over again. Can you imagine eating baked chicken, broccoli, and rice for lunch Monday through Friday? No, thank you!

When I create the meal plan for our weekly meal prep, I make sure that my family and I won't be bored eating the food that we cook for the week. We eat the same meal combo no more than twice, and that's what you'll do when you cook each week's meal plan in this book. You'll eat two different breakfasts each week—one that's good for two meals and another that's good for three. I've made sure that the breakfast you will eat three times is something you'll absolutely enjoy. All the lunches and dinners are good for two meals, and each week has the right amount of variety to make it look like you're eating different meals, so you'll never be bored.

Your weekly meal plan has details on what dishes to combine for each meal. Not feeling the suggested combo? No problem. You can swap the sides because multiple sides from each week can go with the main dishes. You're free to mix things up and create a unique plate.

Other Common Excuses

Fear of being bored with eating the same meal all week isn't the only excuse people give. Here are some other common excuses people share as reasons they don't meal prep. Do you find yourself using these excuses as well? If you do, I have a solution for each one to help address your concerns!

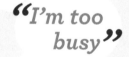

Ah, yes. The age-old excuse that we use to avoid important or must-do things, including meal prepping. We all live fast-paced lives and are almost always busy juggling numerous things. But ask yourself this: Is having healthy meals readily available each week important to you? If you answer "yes," then set aside time to do it, even if you can give the task just one to two hours a week. Make time for what is important.

The amount of work will depend on the complexity of the recipes you're cooking. Pick two or three recipes to start with; I suggest recipes with no more than ten ingredients that you can cook in one pan on the stove or on a sheet pan in the oven. When I'm in a time crunch, I grab two different types of protein, usually chicken and steak, and season them liberally with good-quality spices, such as my favorite and Will's favorite, Greek and Savory blends from Balanced Bites, respectively. (See the "Recommended Products, Brands, and Resources" on page 304 for information about Balanced Bites.) A quick pan-sear and, voilà, protein ready!

"It's a lot of work"

"I don't like leftovers"

Newsflash, my friend: Meal-prepped foods aren't leftovers because you prep and cook them all at once and then store them. They're not meals that are made and served, get picked over by you and your family, and then get refrigerated so someone can eat them again the next day. Sure, each plate you prepare requires reheating, but reheating alone doesn't equate to leftovers. I suggest you reheat them in a cast-iron pan or skillet rather than in the microwave, which can heat food unevenly and dry it out. Reheating on the stove will make the meals taste and look like you just cooked them.

Ending up with the wrong amount of food is a common problem the first few times you meal prep. For example, a recipe that is marked as four servings may not be enough for a family with two growing teenagers.

"I end up prepping too much (or not enough) food"

On the other hand, sometimes you make the right amount of food for eating at home every night, but as the week progresses, you realize there are family events or prior commitments that result in eating out instead of eating your home-cooked meals. I don't suggest freezing the meals at this point because they're no longer freshly cooked. You'll just have to throw away some meals. One of the action items in each week's Meal Prep Game Plan is to plan your week and your meals away from home so you don't cook too much food.

Most of the recipes in this book serve two people per meal, so you'll have to adjust based on the number of family members you're feeding. In the "Deep Dive into Your Weekly Meal Prep Plan" section, I've included a nifty table (page 33) to help you calculate the total number of servings you'll need.

"I don't know where to start"

"It's confusing and overwhelming"

Meal prepping can be daunting whether you're a novice or an expert cook. Cooking multiple meals in one day for the entire week takes a lot of planning. Luckily for you, I've done the heavy lifting and provided all the materials you need to get started on the next four weeks of meal prepping. Just print your meal plan, grocery list, and Meal Prep Game Plan from **easyketomealprep.com**, shop for ingredients, and get ready to whip up all that delicious food in your kitchen!

MEAL PREP SHORTCUTS

In this day and age when new products and technology are introduced left and right to keep up with our fast-paced lifestyles, we can find all kinds of solutions for making the things we do easier. Incorporating these simple shortcuts will make such a big difference when you prep.

Use Precut Veggies

In two or three hours of meal prep, you'll usually spend the majority of your time on peeling, chopping, dicing, and preparing the ingredients to be cooked. I aim to use whole, fresh ingredients whenever I can, so I take the time to prep everything I need beforehand. When

I'm more pressed for time and I need the meal prep to go quickly, I use precut fresh vegetables. Sure, they cost a little bit more, but the price is worth the convenience they provide. More and more grocery stores now carry bags of ready-to-use riced cauliflower, spiralized zucchini, spiralized carrots, butternut squash ribbons, and stir-fry veggies!

I also use a lot of onions and garlic when I cook, so sometimes I grab bags of chopped onions and peeled garlic cloves.

Ask Your Butcher

Butchers at any grocery store will cut or slice your meat for you. Need your flank steak thinly sliced? Some sirloin cubed? Chicken thighs deboned? A whole chicken cut up? They can do anything! Just ask, and they will do it.

When you're grocery shopping, first drop by the meat counter to place your order. Then you can shop while the butcher prepares everything you need. Once you're done, pick up your items and head to the checkout lane. It saves time both while you're grocery shopping and when you're about to cook your meals.

Get Ready-to-Use Essentials

Homemade is always best, but when you're in a pinch, ready-to-use sauces and condiments are time-savers. Salsa, pico de gallo, pesto, and chimichurri are great to make from scratch, but if you're looking for shortcuts, you can grab the ready-made versions. Just make sure the ingredients are clean and have no hidden additives!

Eat Frozen Prepared Meals

No, I'm not talking about those sodium-laden meals from the freezer section of the grocery store! These prepared meals are extra portions that you've made and frozen during your previous meal prep weeks. They're the perfect meal prep shortcut because all you need to do is defrost a meal, reheat it, and prep a quick side for it!

Check out the next section, "Freezing Extra Meals," to learn more about how to properly store cooked meals in the freezer.

FREEZING EXTRA MEALS

I always have at least a couple of frozen, ready-to-eat meals stashed in the freezer for those days when I've been unable to meal prep during the weekend. Doing this doesn't take any extra work; I just double a recipe or two that I'm preparing on meal prep day and then freeze half. Sometimes I cook a recipe that makes more than four servings so I can pack up the extra portions to freeze.

How to Freeze Meals

STEP 1

Let cooked food cool at room temperature for 10 to 15 minutes.

It's perfectly fine to refrigerate food while it's still warm as long as it's not piping hot. Transferring cooked food to a glass container and letting it cool for 10 to 15 minutes before covering will prevent it from steaming in the storage container and producing excess liquid. I learned this lesson when I used to refrigerate hot food immediately; the container would have all this extra water in it when I opened it. When that happens, the food is perfectly fine, but the extra liquid can turn vegetables into a soggy mess and dilute the flavor of the dish.

STEP 2

Store food in vacuum-sealed or zip-top freezer bags.

Using a vacuum food sealer is a great way to seal food before you freeze it. You can build a custom-sized bag to fit the size and quantity of the food that will go in it. The advantage to vacuum-sealed food is that you can store it longer because you've removed all the excess air, which prevents ice crystals or freezer burns from forming.

If you don't have a vacuum sealer, zip-top freezer bags are a good alternative. I still find myself reaching for zip-top bags most of the time because they're more affordable and easier to use than the vacuum sealer. Just remember that the storage life is shorter for food frozen in zip-top bags.

Whether you're using a vacuum sealer or zip-top freezer bags, it's important to remove as much air as possible and store the bag flat to save space in the freezer. Flattening the bag also allows food to freeze and thaw evenly in a shorter period—no need to wrestle with a big chunk of frozen sauce when you're heating it. If you store it flat, all you need to do is break it into pieces that fit in a saucepan and let it simmer. (Make sure to stir it every now and then.)

STEP 3

Label and date each bag.

I can't tell you how many times I've found a bag of food in the freezer, but I had no clue what was in it or how long it had been in there, so I ended up throwing it in the trash! Now I label every item that goes in the freezer with the name of the dish and the date I cooked and packed it, so food does not go to waste. It's also helpful to add the number of servings and any special instructions (example: what food it pairs with or if it's spicy) to clue you in weeks or months later when you're pulling that frozen meal from the freezer.

October 3

Freezer-Friendly Recipes in Easy Keto Meal Prep

Here is a bird's-eye view of the freezable recipes in this book. With each recipe I've given specific freezing instructions for you to follow.

RECIPE	TYPE	NUMBER OF SERVINGS	STORAGE TIME	PAGE NUMBER
Will's Favorite Beef Tapa	Main Dish	4	2 months	56
Chimichurri Pork Chops	Main Dish	4	2 months	58
Sheet Pan Beef and Veggie Kabobs	Main Dish	4	2 months	60
Everything Baked Chicken	Main Dish	4	1 month	62
Weeknight Bolognese	Main Dish	4	2 months	64
Chimichurri	Condiment	About 1 cup	2 months	72
Turkey Mushroom Sauté	Main Dish	4	2 months	94
Crispy Carnitas	Main Dish	4	3 months	96
Pesto Meatballs	Main Dish	8	2 months	98
Carne Asada	Main Dish	8	3 months	100
Chicken Adobo	Main Dish	8	3 months	102
Filipino Turbo Chicken	Main Dish	4	3 months	138
Wonton Noodle Soup	Main Dish	4	2 months	140
Instant Pot Roast	Main Dish	8	3 months	146
Blender Pancakes	Main Dish	6	2 months	178
Five-Spice Meatballs	Main Dish	4	2 months	182
Chicken Korma	Main Dish	4	2 months	184
Instant Pot Beef Barbacoa	Main Dish	4	2 months	186
Easiest Lasagna	Main Dish	8	1 month	188

Thawing Frozen Meals

I recommend two methods for thawing frozen meals to ensure that the food thaws safely:

- Move the bag or container of frozen food from the freezer to the refrigerator the night before you'll be using it. Place it on a plate to catch any liquid that leaks from the bag as the food thaws.

- Submerge the bag of frozen food in a large bowl of cold water. Place it in the refrigerator and replace the water every 30 minutes. It will take 1 to 2 hours to thaw, depending on the quantity.

Never thaw meals by placing them on the counter for any length of time! As soon as food starts to defrost and its temperature goes higher than 40°F, bacteria will multiply.

I know that thawing using the microwave is another option, but that method has a tendency to thaw food unevenly, so I don't recommend it.

TOOLS, GADGETS, AND CONTAINERS

There are a *ton* of nifty tools and gadgets available nowadays, but you just need a few basic tools for meal prepping. I've had a lot of my tools for close to ten years, and they're still holding up pretty well with weekly (and sometimes daily) use. I hand-wash most of these items rather than throwing them in the dishwasher, which helps prolong their longevity. You'll find yourself reaching for these tools often as you go through your weekly meal preps! For the brands that I use and recommend, head to the "Recommended Products, Brands, and Resources" section on page 304.

Must-Have Tools

Can Opener

It's always good to have a can opener in your kitchen drawer because you'll need it to open cans of coconut milk and other canned ingredients for these recipes. No need to spring for a fancy electric opener—a basic manual can opener with a sharp cutting wheel is better, and it'll last longer.

Citrus Squeezer

Get every last bit of lemon or lime juice from the fruit by using a manual citrus squeezer. As a bonus, the squeezer keeps the unwanted seeds from mixing with the juice, so you can throw them away when you discard the citrus peels.

Colander

A colander helps keep multiple vegetables together as you rinse them under running water. The veggies can drain and dry without being individually wiped.

Garlic Press

Another one of my well-used tools for meal prepping is a metal garlic press. You can prepare an entire batch of minced garlic to use in multiple recipes with this handy tool. It rinses easily and doesn't retain the odor of garlic.

Knife Sharpener

My mom gave me an electric knife sharpener as a gift one Christmas, and it was one of the best presents ever. Using a sharpening steel (you know, that metal rod that comes with a knife set) is okay, but it doesn't sharpen and reshape a knife the way an electric sharpener can. A knife is a tool you will use often, so you want to take care of it. If you can't justify an electric sharpener, take your knives to a local place that can professionally sharpen them for you. For example, the farmers market I go to here in Long Beach, California, has a stall that offers knife-sharpening services. Remember, a sharp knife is a safe knife!

Knives

If I were to pick just two knives to have in my drawer, my choices would be the Zwilling 9-inch chef's knife and 7-inch santoku knife. Both knives feel solid in my hand without being heavy, so I never worry that I'll end up slicing myself. I find myself reaching for one or the other when I'm cooking, and both are great for chopping and slicing vegetables as well as cutting meat. Dull knives are a no-no; in fact, they're more dangerous to use than sharp knives because of the extra amount of pressure you need to apply to the blade to cut. Regularly sharpening keeps your knives in tip-top condition.

Measuring Cups and Spoons

My heavy-duty metal measuring cups and spoons are some of my most-used tools. They work for both liquid and dry ingredients, and they can double as small condiment containers during prepping. The measuring cup set should have 1 cup, ½ cup, ⅓ cup, and ¼ cup sizes, and the measuring spoon set should include at least these sizes: 1 tablespoon, 1 teaspoon, ½ teaspoon, and ¼ teaspoon.

Meat Thermometer

I highly recommend a meat thermometer to help you avoid overcooking your food. Get one that you can program for the type of meat you're cooking, and say goodbye to tough, leathery steaks or dry chicken.

Microplane Zester

I use a Microplane zester not only for citrus ingredients but also for grating ginger and hard cheeses such as Parmesan. If you don't have a garlic press, you also can use this tool to mince garlic—just be careful because garlic cloves are tiny, and the blades are sharp!

To get every last bit of food out of the blades when cleaning the Microplane zester, use a toothbrush to scrub the it under water.

Mixing Bowls

Having a set of small, medium, and large bowls (either glass or stainless) is a big help when meal prepping ingredients, especially large amounts of vegetables. A bowl also can double as an ice bath or double boiler.

Mortar and Pestle

Sometimes a food processor is too big for the amount of an ingredient that you need to prepare (a tablespoon of crushed peppercorns, anyone?), so it's nice to have a mortar and pestle handy to crush small amounts of hard nuts or spices by giving them a good whack.

Splatter Guard

Foods that have a high water content tend to splatter when they come in contact with hot oil. Prevent an oily disaster all over your stove, backsplash, clothes, or (worst) arm by using a splatter guard when you're pan-frying.

Tongs

A good pair (or two) of tongs comes in handy for many cooking tasks. Tongs provide a solid clamp on food, and they're my preferred tool to use when flipping steak or frying small foods, such as shrimp or chicken tenders. Sometimes I even use tongs when sautéing vegetables because they give me better leverage to quickly flip the veggies without making a mess.

Vegetable Peeler

Either a swivel or a fixed-blade vegetable peeler is essential for prepping vegetables quickly. I prefer the swivel blade because it adapts to the shape of any vegetable, which makes peeling a breeze. I also use the peeler to remove the thin skin from ginger before grating it and to shave blocks of hard cheese.

Whisk

A small metal whisk isn't just for beating eggs. It also works great for blending ingredients to make smooth and lump-free dressings and dips.

Wooden Chopping Board

I have a giant 24 by 32-inch butcher's block beauty that was custom-made for me by my friend Katie Cordoza. This chopping board makes prepping a whole bunch of ingredients super easy because I have so much cutting space! Aside from that, I use a smaller 18 by 12-inch butcher's block that is dedicated solely to cutting raw meat. I'm very wary of cross-contamination when it comes to food, so I always make sure I have two separate chopping boards; I clean and sanitize each one after use.

> *I don't recommend using plastic cutting boards. Bacteria can sink deep into the grooves where the knife meets the plastic. Good-quality wooden boards can better withstand sharp knives, so there are fewer grooves, which means less space for bacteria to hide.*

Wooden and Silicone Spoons and Spatulas

Cooking with both wooden and silicone spoons and spatulas is so much better than cooking with plastic utensils. Both can withstand high temperatures and are BPA-free.

Must-Have Equipment

Baking Dish

A baking dish is perfect for meal-prepped casseroles, so it's handy to have at least one on hand. You can bake any protein in it to catch liquid that's produced during cooking. The recipes in this book use one of two sizes of baking dish: 8 by 8-inch square or 11 by 7-inch rectangle.

Blender (Immersion or Regular)

You can use either a regular or an immersion blender to make cauliflower puree, pancake batter, or mayonnaise in just a couple of minutes. A blender also can crush nuts or ice and whip up a frothy matcha drink with just a touch of a button.

Cast-Iron Pan

The majority of dishes in this book call for a large cast-iron pan (10 to 12 inches in diameter) as the cooking vessel. I'm a big fan of this type of pan for its superior heat retention and durability. When preheated well, nothing sticks to the surface, so even sunny-side-up fried eggs slide right off. I swear by the low-maintenance Staub pan that I've had for at least four years because it's easy to clean, and I never have to re-season it!

Digital Food Scale

I use a digital scale when I need precise measurements for almond and coconut flours. A scale's also useful for making meatballs; you can make sure each one weighs the same to ensure even cooking.

Food Processor

A food processor is what I call the *blender's cousin* because it can perform similar tasks, such as grinding and pureeing, but it can perform other functions, too, such as slicing vegetables and grating cheese when you swap the blades.

Glass Food Storage Containers

I have more than a dozen glass containers in different sizes that I use for storing cooked food and packing my breakfasts and lunches to take to work. The Pyrex and Glasslock brands are the most durable ones I've tried, and the following sizes are what you'll need the most for meal prepping: 6 cups, 4 cups, 3 cups, 2 cups, and 1 cup. They're available in both rectangular and circular containers.

Instant Pot

The Instant Pot is one of the best inventions ever, and you can get it for a deeply discounted price on Black Friday. (Check Amazon.com, for example.) I've made a lot of roasts, stews, and less-than-thirty-minute meals in the Instant Pot. I have two models: the LUX60 and the DUO60. Both have six-quart pots, which is perfect for a family of four to six people.

Jars

A set of jars such as 1-pint and ½-pint mason jars are perfect for storing soups, sauces, and condiments. They're freezer-friendly, so you can portion out one or two servings per jar and transfer them to the freezer for future meals.

Rimmed Baking Sheets

From cookies to sheet-pan dinners and roasting vegetables, a rimmed baking sheet is what I reach for most of the time when I'm cooking food in the oven. Lining the pan with parchment paper or foil prevents baked bits of food from getting stuck, which makes cleanup easier.

Saucepans

A saucepan is for soups, sauces, and other dishes that you cook with liquid. I use a small pan for melting butter, a medium pan for reheating meals, and a large pan for making soups and blanching vegetables.

Stainless Skillet

A large stainless skillet (10 to 12 inches in diameter) is another kitchen workhorse that you can use to cook almost anything. I love to sear steak in my All-Clad d5 pan because I get a beautiful golden brown crust on the outside while the meat stays tender on the inside. I also use the skillet for sautéing vegetables so they stay crisp. All-Clad skillets are well built and will last for many years.

Stand Mixer or Hand Mixer

A mixer is a splurge item. I use it mostly for baked recipes, but you also can use it with a flat beater attachment for shredding cooked meat, such as Crispy Carnitas (page 96) and Instant Pot Roast (page 146). I have an attachment for my stand mixer that transforms it into a vegetable spiralizer, so I can make big batches of zucchini noodles (zoodles) to eat with my Weeknight Bolognese (page 64).

PANTRY ESSENTIALS

These pantry essentials are ingredients you'll use in a number of recipes in the four weeks' worth of meal plans in this book. Make sure to stock up so you have enough of each one on hand. You have the option to buy these items ahead of time before shopping for the ingredients you need for the first meal plan, or you can buy these pantry essentials every week.

Each week's grocery list has an In Your Pantry category that lists how much of each pantry essential you will need for the week. If you're running low on an ingredient, mark that pantry item on your shopping list to replenish it.

Visit **easyketomealprep.com/pantry** to print the downloadable Pantry Essentials checklist.

Avocado oil, 2 (500-ml) bottles

Ghee, 2 (9-ounce) jars

Olive oil, extra-virgin, 3 (500-ml) bottles

Olive oil spray, 1 (5-ounce) can

Apple cider vinegar, 1 (16-ounce) bottle

Balsamic vinegar, 1 (8-ounce) bottle

Broth, beef, 1 (16-ounce) carton

Broth, chicken, 1 (16-ounce) carton

Coconut aminos, 3 (8½-ounce) bottles

Coconut milk, full-fat, 4 (13½-ounce) cans

Fish sauce, 1 (8½-ounce) bottle

Toasted sesame oil, 1 (5-ounce) bottle

Bay leaves, 1 (0.15-ounce) jar

Black pepper, 1 (2½-ounce) jar

Fine sea salt 1 (2½-ounce) jar

Garlic powder, 1 (2-ounce) jar

Ground cumin, 1 (1-ounce) jar

Ground dried oregano, 1 (½-ounce) jar

Onion powder, 1 (2-ounce) jar

Paprika, 1 (2-ounce) jar

Red pepper flakes, 1 (1-ounce) jar

DEEP DIVE INTO YOUR WEEKLY MEAL PREP PLAN

Before you get started, you need to familiarize yourself with the components of the weekly meal prep plans.

Getting Started

Each week begins with a brief overview of the kinds of recipes you'll be preparing and cooking. Whether you're a beginner or a seasoned meal prepper, weeks 1 and 2 are easier in terms of the number of ingredients and the amount of prep work involved. Weeks 3 and 4 are intermediate; I introduce multiple cooking methods that you can use simultaneously to maximize your time in the kitchen.

WEEK 1

Getting Started

Welcome to week 1 of meal prepping! I'm sure you're pumped to get started. Make sure you've reviewed the Deep Dive into Your Weekly Meal Prep Plan section (pages 31 to 39) so you know what to expect. If this is your first attempt at meal prepping keto meals, don't stress! The menu is simple, and the recipes are easy to make.

Take advantage of the Prep Time-Savers to cut down on prep time. These are listed in the grocery list and in some of the recipes.

Print the downloadable week 1 PDF from **easyketomealprep.com/week1.**

I also provide the link to the downloadable PDF for the week that contains the meal plan, grocery list, and Meal Prep Game Plan in case you'd like to print them out, mark them up with notes, and have a shopping list that you can take with you to the grocery store.

What's on the Menu

This section gives you an overview of the entire menu for the week, including the cooking methods you'll use, the estimated prep and cook times, and the number of servings in each recipe.

The majority of recipes you will cook yields four servings, which feeds two people because each recipe is a component of two meals for the week. Some recipes yield eight servings, so you can freeze half to eat at another time.

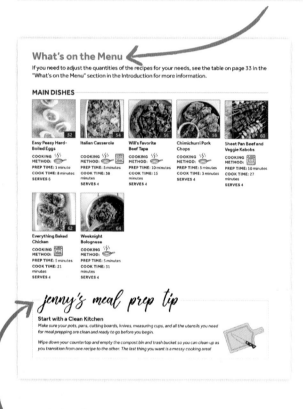

Jenny's Weekly Meal Prep Tip

I give you a useful meal prep tip each week to get you in the groove of meal prepping!

Save Half for Later

Some recipes make more food than you will need for the week. These notes tell you which recipes make extra food that you can freeze for future meals.

If you're cooking for just yourself or for a family of four or more and need to adjust the quantity of the meals, you'll need to make ingredient modifications for each recipe. Because I want to make meal prep super easy for you, I've done the math so you don't have to! As you're prepping for each week, go over the recipes you'll be making. Refer to this table to adjust for the number of meals you need to serve only yourself or your larger family.

# OF PEOPLE TO FEED	RECIPE SERVES	MULTIPLY BY	DIVIDE BY	TOTAL # OF SERVINGS
1	4	-	2	2
1	8	-	4	2
2	4	-	-	4
2	8	-	2	4
4	4	2	-	8
4	8	-	-	8
6	4	3	-	12
6	8	1.5	-	12
8	4	4	-	16
8	8	2	-	16

If you want to freeze extra servings of a recipe, you may opt not to halve recipes if you're cooking for one, or you may need to double the number you are using so you can make a larger quantity for a family of four or more.

It's helpful to refer to this information as you follow the Meal Prep Game Plan, and there's an option for you to print the weekly menu on **easyketomealprep.com** so you can stick it to your kitchen cabinet or refrigerator. You can use the printed menu to track your progress and cross out items after you've prepped and cooked them.

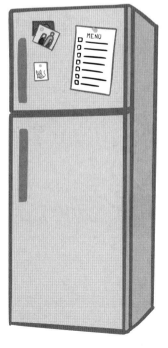

Meal Plan

We all have preferences when it comes to meal prepping. I like to get everything done on the weekend so throughout the week I can enjoy all the ready-to-eat meals that I have available in the refrigerator. Sometimes I pretend that I'm at a buffet as I open my fridge and figure out what to eat for my next meal. I like having a lot of options that I can mix and match so I don't get bored eating the same meal multiple times a week. Each of the four weekly meal plans in this book contains a variety of recipes, so you will eat the same meal no more than two or three times during the week.

One of the things that you'll notice about meal prepping on a keto diet is that you will cook fewer recipes because you don't need to prepare starchy carbohydrates (such as rice and potatoes) to eat with each meal. That means each plate you put together will have a good amount of protein and fats and a generous serving of vegetables. Gotta have those veggies! They are packed with vitamins and minerals and will keep you full and satisfied longer.

You have a few options to choose from when you're meal prepping each week.

Cook Once a Week

If you're the type of person who prefers to get everything done in one day, then cooking once a week is for you. Block out a good amount of time—three to four hours—to get everything cooked and the kitchen cleaned. To make meal prepping go faster, have your significant other or older children help out. I meal prep once a week, and having Will on ingredient prep and dish duty has been a huge time-saver! It's super fun, too, because we listen to a couple of our playlists of meal prep jams while we work together.

Cooking once a week means less stress in figuring out what to eat each day, especially on those nights when you come home tired and really hungry.

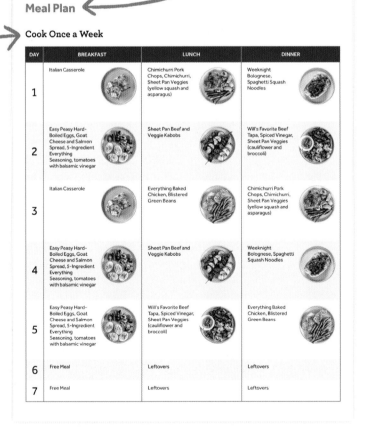

Meal Plan

Cook Once a Week

DAY	BREAKFAST	LUNCH	DINNER
1	Italian Casserole	Chimichurri Pork Chops, Chimichurri, Sheet Pan Veggies (yellow squash and asparagus)	Weeknight Bolognese, Spaghetti Squash Noodles
2	Easy Peasy Hard-Boiled Eggs, Goat Cheese and Salmon Spread, 5-Ingredient Everything Seasoning, tomatoes with balsamic vinegar	Sheet Pan Beef and Veggie Kabobs	Will's Favorite Beef Tapa, Spiced Vinegar, Sheet Pan Veggies (cauliflower and broccoli)
3	Italian Casserole	Everything Baked Chicken, Blistered Green Beans	Chimichurri Pork Chops, Chimichurri, Sheet Pan Veggies (yellow squash and asparagus)
4	Easy Peasy Hard-Boiled Eggs, Goat Cheese and Salmon Spread, 5-Ingredient Everything Seasoning, tomatoes with balsamic vinegar	Sheet Pan Beef and Veggie Kabobs	Weeknight Bolognese, Spaghetti Squash Noodles
5	Easy Peasy Hard-Boiled Eggs, Goat Cheese and Salmon Spread, 5-Ingredient Everything Seasoning, tomatoes with balsamic vinegar	Will's Favorite Beef Tapa, Spiced Vinegar, Sheet Pan Veggies (cauliflower and broccoli)	Everything Baked Chicken, Blistered Green Beans
6	Free Meal	Leftovers	Leftovers
7	Free Meal	Leftovers	Leftovers

Cook Twice a Week

Sometimes cooking only once a week won't work because you have family events or commitments, or maybe you just don't feel like doing an intensive one-day session. Or maybe you're new to the world of meal prepping, and you just want to avoid feeling overwhelmed with cooking everything in one day. If that's the case, you will benefit the most by following the Cook Twice a Week approach. I've broken down the meals for the week into two prep sessions; you cook the first half before day 1 of your upcoming week (usually on the weekend), and you cook the second half midweek, about four days later.

Do It Yourself (DIY)

If you want the freedom and flexibility to combine multiple items into one meal, you can make a DIY plan by downloading the blank meal plan template on **easyketomealprep.com**. The recipes in each of the weekly meal plans complement each other so you can easily make a unique plate.

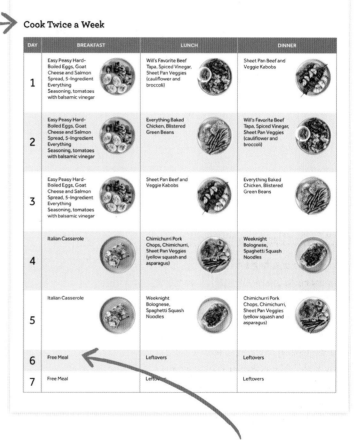

Cook Twice a Week

DAY	BREAKFAST	LUNCH	DINNER
1	Easy Peasy Hard-Boiled Eggs, Goat Cheese and Salmon Spread, 5-Ingredient Everything Seasoning, tomatoes with balsamic vinegar	Will's Favorite Beef Tapa, Spiced Vinegar, Sheet Pan Veggies (cauliflower and broccoli)	Sheet Pan Beef and Veggie Kabobs
2	Easy Peasy Hard-Boiled Eggs, Goat Cheese and Salmon Spread, 5-Ingredient Everything Seasoning, tomatoes with balsamic vinegar	Everything Baked Chicken, Blistered Green Beans	Will's Favorite Beef Tapa, Spiced Vinegar, Sheet Pan Veggies (cauliflower and broccoli)
3	Easy Peasy Hard-Boiled Eggs, Goat Cheese and Salmon Spread, 5-Ingredient Everything Seasoning, tomatoes with balsamic vinegar	Sheet Pan Beef and Veggie Kabobs	Everything Baked Chicken, Blistered Green Beans
4	Italian Casserole	Chimichurri Pork Chops, Chimichurri, Sheet Pan Veggies (yellow squash and asparagus)	Weeknight Bolognese, Spaghetti Squash Noodles
5	Italian Casserole	Weeknight Bolognese, Spaghetti Squash Noodles	Chimichurri Pork Chops, Chimichurri, Sheet Pan Veggies (yellow squash and asparagus)
6	Free Meal	Leftovers	Leftovers
7	Free Meal	Leftovers	Leftovers

Free Meals and Leftovers in Your Meal Plan

After doing my meal prep challenges for the past couple of years and gathering feedback from those who have participated, I've learned that each week is different. You might have a work lunch to welcome a new employee, a midweek date night, or a dinner at the in-laws' that takes priority over a prepped meal.

I call these Free Meals, and you can account for them in each week's meal plan. Simply cross out meals on the calendar where you won't be eating a prepped meal. Save the prepped meal for the weekend where meals are marked as Leftovers.

Grocery List

The grocery list is broken down into the following categories: Meat and Seafood, Eggs and Dairy, Produce, Condiments and Spices, Other Items, and Frozen Items (where applicable). The In Your Pantry category includes items that I listed as pantry essentials on page 30; cross out any items that you don't need to buy for the coming week.

There may be a recipe or two where you'll have extra ingredients because convenience food items, such as a bag of cut-up veggies, hold a quantity that's more than what a recipe calls for. If you end up with extra veggies, don't toss them out. At the end of the week, you can quickly blanch or sauté them to have a fresh side to go with a meal.

In the printable grocery list PDFs, I've provided extra space for additional items, such as ingredients for snacks and treats. If you're prepping one of the recipes I've provided in the "Snacks, Treats, and Drink Recipes" section (beginning on page 247), this is where to add the ingredients you need.

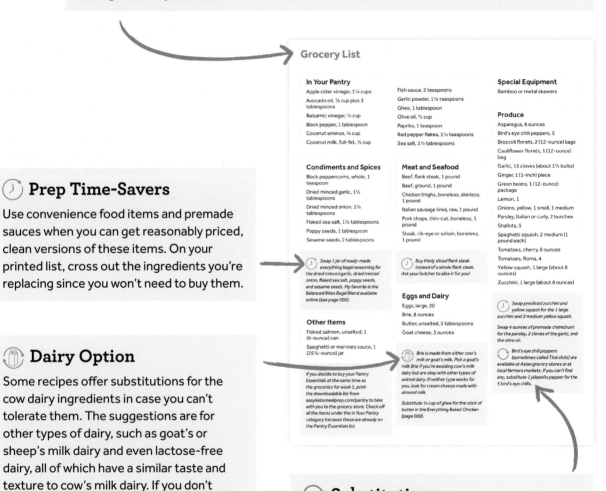

Grocery List

In Your Pantry
Apple cider vinegar, 1¼ cups
Avocado oil, ¼ cup plus 3 tablespoons
Balsamic vinegar, ¼ cup
Black pepper, 1 tablespoon
Coconut aminos, ¼ cup
Coconut milk, full-fat, ⅓ cup

Fish sauce, 2 teaspoons
Garlic powder, 1½ teaspoons
Ghee, 1 tablespoon
Olive oil, ½ cup
Paprika, 1 teaspoon
Red pepper flakes, 1½ teaspoons
Sea salt, 1½ tablespoons

Special Equipment
Bamboo or metal skewers

Produce
Asparagus, 8 ounces
Bird's eye chili peppers, 5
Broccoli florets, 2 (12-ounce) bags
Cauliflower florets, 1 (12-ounce) bag
Garlic, 15 cloves (about 1½ bulbs)
Ginger, 1 (1-inch) piece
Green beans, 1 (12-ounce) package
Lemon, 1
Onions, yellow, 1 small, 1 medium
Parsley, Italian or curly, 2 bunches
Shallots, 5
Spaghetti squash, 2 medium (1 pound each)
Tomatoes, cherry, 8 ounces
Tomatoes, Roma, 4
Yellow squash, 1 large (about 8 ounces)
Zucchini, 1 large (about 8 ounces)

Condiments and Spices
Black peppercorns, whole, 1 teaspoon
Dried minced garlic, 1½ tablespoons
Dried minced onion, 1½ tablespoons
Flaked sea salt, 1½ tablespoons
Poppy seeds, 1 tablespoon
Sesame seeds, 2 tablespoons

Meat and Seafood
Beef, flank steak, 1 pound
Beef, ground, 1 pound
Chicken thighs, boneless, skinless, 1 pound
Italian sausage links, raw, 1 pound
Pork chops, thin-cut, boneless, 1 pound
Steak, rib-eye or sirloin, boneless, 1 pound

Swap 1 jar of ready-made everything bagel seasoning for the dried minced garlic, dried minced onion, flaked sea salt, poppy seeds, and sesame seeds. My favorite is the Balanced Bites Bagel Blend available online (see page 000).

Buy thinly sliced flank steak instead of a whole flank steak. Ask your butcher to slice it for you!

Eggs and Dairy
Eggs, large, 20
Brie, 8 ounces
Butter, unsalted, 5 tablespoons
Goat cheese, 3 ounces

Other Items
Flaked salmon, unsalted, 1 (6-ounce) can
Spaghetti or marinara sauce, 1 (25½-ounce) jar

If you decide to buy your Pantry Essentials at the same time as the groceries for week 1, print the downloadable list from easyketomealprep.com/pantry to take with you to the grocery store. Check off all the items under the In Your Pantry category because these are already on the Pantry Essentials list.

Brie is made from either cow's milk or goat's milk. Pick a goat's milk Brie if you're avoiding cow's milk dairy but are okay with other types of animal dairy. If neither type works for you, look for cream cheese made with almond milk.

Substitute ½ cup of ghee for the stick of butter in the Everything Baked Chicken (page 000).

Swap presliced zucchini and yellow squash for the 1 large zucchini and 2 medium yellow squash.

Swap 4 ounces of premade chimichurri for the parsley, 2 cloves of the garlic, and the olive oil.

Bird's eye chili peppers (sometimes called Thai chilis) are available at Asian grocery stores or at local farmers markets. If you can't find any, substitute 1 jalapeño pepper for the 5 bird's eye chilis.

⏱ Prep Time-Savers

Use convenience food items and premade sauces when you can get reasonably priced, clean versions of these items. On your printed list, cross out the ingredients you're replacing since you won't need to buy them.

🥛 Dairy Option

Some recipes offer substitutions for the cow dairy ingredients in case you can't tolerate them. The suggestions are for other types of dairy, such as goat's or sheep's milk dairy and even lactose-free dairy, all of which have a similar taste and texture to cow's milk dairy. If you don't have any issues with those types of dairy, they make good substitutes. If all types of animal dairy are a no-go for you, nut-based substitutes will work in some recipes.

Substitutions

In some recipes, I offer substitutions you can make to replace items that are sometimes hard to find with more commonly available items.

Meal Prep Game Plan

This is your weekly guide to help you be ready to get cookin' on meal prep day. Some action items in the prep work take only a few minutes, and doing a little bit every day saves time and eliminates stress on meal prep day. I find it's most manageable to distribute the prep work over three days, but you may find that distributing tasks in a different way suits your schedule better.

Here's the template I use for my weekly game plan:

ESTIMATED TIME SPENT: 15 minutes

1. Read and review the week's menu, grocery list, meal plan, and recipes. Print the downloadable PDF for the week.

   If you want to include keto-friendly snacks or treats to your meal plan for the week, add the ingredients you need to the Other Items category of your grocery list. In each week's meal plan, I suggest some options from the "Snacks, Treats, and Drink Recipes" chapter.

2. Review the In Your Pantry section of the grocery list and check off any items that you already have on hand. Be sure you have enough of each pantry item for the recipes you will prepare on meal prep day.

3. Review the Prep Time-Savers, Substitutions, and Dairy Options sections of the grocery list.

   You can buy the convenience items suggested to help cut your prep time this week. Cross off the ingredients that each convenience item replaces on the grocery list.

   Mark ingredients that you need to substitute for; also take note of your preferred dairy option and indicate your choice.

4. Check your calendar for family/work/social events in the coming week. Mark any meals when you won't be eating your prepared dishes. Swap these meals with Leftovers or a Free Meal.

ESTIMATED TIME SPENT: 45 minutes

Shop for groceries. Don't forget your printed grocery list (and Pantry Essentials list if you're shopping for both).

ESTIMATED TIME SPENT: 1 hour

POWER HOUR PREP

Prepare sauces and seasonings, veggies that need to be prepped, and aromatics that you'll use in the majority of recipes for the week. Preparing everything that you need at one time makes cooking easier. This step is crucial, so make sure you don't skip it!

Recipes

Each recipe lists the number of servings, prep time, and cook time. You also can find that information in the What's on the Menu section.

All recipes are for two adults to eat twice except for one breakfast meal that makes up three meals. Recipes that serve eight make extra that you can freeze to eat later.

The allergen information is clearly stated on each recipe:

- Dairy-free
- Egg-free
- Nut-free

Of course, everything is free of gluten, wheat, and soy, so you don't need to worry about those allergens!

Each recipe includes storage and reheating instructions:

- Refrigerating
- Freezing
- Reheating from frozen
- Storing in the pantry

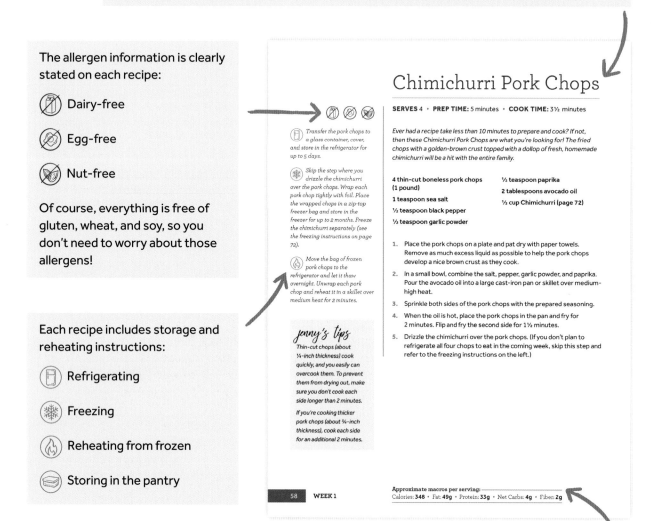

Chimichurri Pork Chops

SERVES 4 • **PREP TIME:** 5 minutes • **COOK TIME:** 3½ minutes

Ever had a recipe take less than 10 minutes to prepare and cook? If not, then these Chimichurri Pork Chops are what you're looking for! The fried chops with a golden-brown crust topped with a dollop of fresh, homemade chimichurri will be a hit with the entire family.

4 thin-cut boneless pork chops (1 pound)

1 teaspoon sea salt

½ teaspoon black pepper

½ teaspoon garlic powder

½ teaspoon paprika

2 tablespoons avocado oil

½ cup Chimichurri (page 72)

1. Place the pork chops on a plate and pat dry with paper towels. Remove as much excess liquid as possible to help the pork chops develop a nice brown crust as they cook.

2. In a small bowl, combine the salt, pepper, garlic powder, and paprika. Pour the avocado oil into a large cast-iron pan or skillet over medium-high heat.

3. Sprinkle both sides of the pork chops with the prepared seasoning.

4. When the oil is hot, place the pork chops in the pan and fry for 2 minutes. Flip and fry the second side for 1½ minutes.

5. Drizzle the chimichurri over the pork chops. (If you don't plan to refrigerate all four chops to eat in the coming week, skip this step and refer to the freezing instructions on the left.)

Transfer the pork chops to a glass container, cover, and store in the refrigerator for up to 5 days.

Skip the step where you drizzle the chimichurri over the pork chops. Wrap each pork chop tightly with foil. Place the wrapped chops in a zip-top freezer bag and store in the freezer for up to 2 months. Freeze the chimichurri separately (see the freezing instructions on page 72).

Move the bag of frozen pork chops to the refrigerator and let it thaw overnight. Unwrap each pork chop and reheat it in a skillet over medium heat for 2 minutes.

jenny's tips

Thin-cut chops (about ¼-inch thickness) cook quickly, and you easily can overcook them. To prevent them from drying out, make sure you don't cook each side longer than 2 minutes.

If you're cooking thicker pork chops (about ¼-inch thickness), cook each side for an additional 2 minutes.

Approximate macros per serving:
Calories: **348** • Fat: **49g** • Protein: **33g** • Net Carbs: **4g** • Fiber: **2g**

58   WEEK 1

Each recipe also includes a macro calculation (Calories/Fat/Protein/Net Carbs/Fiber) per serving. See the "What's the Deal with Net Carbs?" sidebar on page 16 for more information about net carbs versus total carbs.

My Meal Prep Notes

This is a blank area for you to write notes to yourself about each week's prep: what challenges you encountered, what your favorite recipe was, what substitutions you used, how you felt about meal prepping this week, how long it took you—pretty much anything you want to remember later! Feel free to scribble notes and comments in any section of your book. I know it may not feel right to do this, but your copy will look and feel well loved when you write on it!

My Week 3 Meal Prep Notes

Build Your Plate

Each week has two set meal plans with different recipe combinations for each weekday meal: one for the Cook Once a Week approach and one for the Cook Twice a Week approach. Since all meals are prepped ahead of time and refrigerated, you will need to spend no more than five minutes plating and reheating what you're scheduled to eat. Follow the reheating instructions and plating guide presented in this section to build your perfect plate.

Easy Peasy Hard-Boiled Eggs, Goat Cheese and Salmon Spread, 5-Ingredient Everything Seasoning, cherry and grape tomatoes with balsamic vinegar

1. Boil 3 cups of water and pour it into a large bowl. Grab 4 hard-boiled eggs from the refrigerator and place them in the hot water for 5 minutes to warm them.

2. Cut the eggs in half and divide them between two plates.

3. Top each egg with 1 tablespoon of Goat Cheese and Salmon Spread (page 73).

4. Sprinkle with 1 tablespoon of 5-Ingredient Everything Seasoning (page 75).

5. Halve the assorted cherry and grape tomatoes and divide them between the two plates.

6. Drizzle 1 tablespoon of balsamic vinegar on the tomatoes and season them with a pinch of salt and pepper.

Part 2: 4 Weekly
done-for-you Plans

WEEK 1

Getting Started

Welcome to week 1 of meal prepping! I'm sure you're pumped to get started. Make sure you've reviewed the Deep Dive into Your Weekly Meal Prep Plan section (pages 31 to 39) so you know what to expect. If this is your first attempt at meal prepping keto meals, don't stress! The menu is simple, and the recipes are easy to make.

Take advantage of the Prep Time-Savers to cut down on prep time. These are listed in the grocery list and in some of the recipes.

Print the downloadable week 1 PDF from **easyketomealprep.com/week1.**

What's on the Menu

If you need to adjust the quantities of the recipes for your needs, see the table on page 33 in the "What's on the Menu" section in the Introduction for more information.

MAIN DISHES

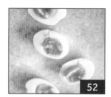
Easy Peasy Hard-Boiled Eggs

COOKING METHOD:
PREP TIME: 1 minute
COOK TIME: 8 minutes
SERVES 6

Italian Casserole

COOKING METHOD:
PREP TIME: 5 minutes
COOK TIME: 38 minutes
SERVES 4

Will's Favorite Beef Tapa

COOKING METHOD:
PREP TIME: 10 minutes
COOK TIME: 15 minutes
SERVES 4

Chimichurri Pork Chops

COOKING METHOD:
PREP TIME: 5 minutes
COOK TIME: 3 minutes
SERVES 4

Sheet Pan Beef and Veggie Kabobs

COOKING METHOD:
PREP TIME: 10 minutes
COOK TIME: 27 minutes
SERVES 4

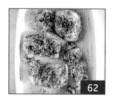
Everything Baked Chicken

COOKING METHOD:
PREP TIME: 5 minutes
COOK TIME: 21 minutes
SERVES 4

Weeknight Bolognese

COOKING METHOD:
PREP TIME: 5 minutes
COOK TIME: 31 minutes
SERVES 4

jenny's meal prep tip

Start with a Clean Kitchen

Make sure your pots, pans, cutting boards, knives, measuring cups, and all the utensils you need for meal prepping are clean and ready to go before you begin.

Wipe down your countertop and empty the compost bin and trash bucket so you can clean up as you transition from one recipe to the other. The last thing you want is a messy cooking area!

SIDES

Blistered Green Beans

COOKING METHOD:

PREP TIME: 10 minutes

COOK TIME: 11 minutes

SERVES 4

Spaghetti Squash Noodles

COOKING METHOD:

PREP TIME: 2 minutes

COOK TIME: 35 minutes

SERVES 4

Sheet Pan Veggies

COOKING METHOD:

PREP TIME: 5 minutes

COOK TIME: 20 minutes

SERVES 4

CONDIMENTS AND GARNISHES

Chimichurri

COOKING METHOD: —

PREP TIME: 15 minutes

COOK TIME: —

YIELD: 1 cup

Goat Cheese and Salmon Spread

COOKING METHOD: —

PREP TIME: 5 minutes

COOK TIME: —

YIELD: 1 cup

Spiced Vinegar

COOKING METHOD: —

PREP TIME: 5 minutes

COOK TIME: —

YIELD: 1 cup

5-Ingredient Everything Seasoning

COOKING METHOD: —

PREP TIME: 5 minutes

COOK TIME: —

YIELD: ½ cup

Assorted cherry and grape tomatoes

Balsamic vinegar

save half for later

The Chimichurri recipe (page 72) makes a generous portion, so freeze any extras to use later. The freezing instructions are in the ❄ Freeze This section of the recipe.

Meal Plan

Cook Once a Week

DAY	BREAKFAST	LUNCH	DINNER
1	Italian Casserole	Chimichurri Pork Chops, Chimichurri, Sheet Pan Veggies (yellow squash and asparagus)	Weeknight Bolognese, Spaghetti Squash Noodles
2	Easy Peasy Hard-Boiled Eggs, Goat Cheese and Salmon Spread, 5-Ingredient Everything Seasoning, tomatoes with balsamic vinegar	Sheet Pan Beef and Veggie Kabobs	Will's Favorite Beef Tapa, Spiced Vinegar, Sheet Pan Veggies (cauliflower and broccoli)
3	Italian Casserole	Everything Baked Chicken, Blistered Green Beans	Chimichurri Pork Chops, Chimichurri, Sheet Pan Veggies (yellow squash and asparagus)
4	Easy Peasy Hard-Boiled Eggs, Goat Cheese and Salmon Spread, 5-Ingredient Everything Seasoning, tomatoes with balsamic vinegar	Sheet Pan Beef and Veggie Kabobs	Weeknight Bolognese, Spaghetti Squash Noodles
5	Easy Peasy Hard-Boiled Eggs, Goat Cheese and Salmon Spread, 5-Ingredient Everything Seasoning, tomatoes with balsamic vinegar	Will's Favorite Beef Tapa, Spiced Vinegar, Sheet Pan Veggies (cauliflower and broccoli)	Everything Baked Chicken, Blistered Green Beans
6	Free Meal	Leftovers	Leftovers
7	Free Meal	Leftovers	Leftovers

Cook Twice a Week

DAY	BREAKFAST	LUNCH	DINNER
1	Easy Peasy Hard-Boiled Eggs, Goat Cheese and Salmon Spread, 5-Ingredient Everything Seasoning, tomatoes with balsamic vinegar	Will's Favorite Beef Tapa, Spiced Vinegar, Sheet Pan Veggies (cauliflower and broccoli)	Sheet Pan Beef and Veggie Kabobs
2	Easy Peasy Hard-Boiled Eggs, Goat Cheese and Salmon Spread, 5-Ingredient Everything Seasoning, tomatoes with balsamic vinegar	Everything Baked Chicken, Blistered Green Beans	Will's Favorite Beef Tapa, Spiced Vinegar, Sheet Pan Veggies (cauliflower and broccoli)
3	Easy Peasy Hard-Boiled Eggs, Goat Cheese and Salmon Spread, 5-Ingredient Everything Seasoning, tomatoes with balsamic vinegar	Sheet Pan Beef and Veggie Kabobs	Everything Baked Chicken, Blistered Green Beans
4	Italian Casserole	Chimichurri Pork Chops, Chimichurri, Sheet Pan Veggies (yellow squash and asparagus)	Weeknight Bolognese, Spaghetti Squash Noodles
5	Italian Casserole	Weeknight Bolognese, Spaghetti Squash Noodles	Chimichurri Pork Chops, Chimichurri, Sheet Pan Veggies (yellow squash and asparagus)
6	Free Meal	Leftovers	Leftovers
7	Free Meal	Leftovers	Leftovers

Grocery List

In Your Pantry

Apple cider vinegar, 1¼ cups

Avocado oil, ¼ cup plus 3 tablespoons

Balsamic vinegar, ¼ cup

Black pepper, 1 tablespoon

Coconut aminos, ¾ cup

Coconut milk, full-fat, ½ cup

Fish sauce, 2 teaspoons

Garlic powder, 1½ teaspoons

Ghee, 1 tablespoon

Olive oil, ½ cup

Paprika, 1 teaspoon

Red pepper flakes, 1½ teaspoons

Sea salt, 1½ tablespoons

Condiments and Spices

Black peppercorns, whole, 1 teaspoon

Dried minced garlic, 1½ tablespoons

Dried minced onion, 1½ tablespoons

Flaked sea salt, 1½ tablespoons

Poppy seeds, 1 tablespoon

Sesame seeds, 2 tablespoons

🕐 *Swap 1 jar of ready-made everything bagel seasoning for the dried minced garlic, dried minced onion, flaked sea salt, poppy seeds, and sesame seeds. My favorite is the Balanced Bites Bagel Blend available online (see page 304).*

Other Items

Flaked salmon, unsalted, 1 (6-ounce) can

Spaghetti or marinara sauce, 1 (25½-ounce) jar

If you decide to buy your Pantry Essentials at the same time as the groceries for week 1, print the downloadable list from easyketomealprep.com/pantry to take with you to the grocery store. Check off all the items under the In Your Pantry category because these are already on the Pantry Essentials list.

Meat and Seafood

Beef, flank steak, 1 pound

Beef, ground, 1 pound

Chicken thighs, boneless, skinless, 1 pound

Italian sausage links, raw, 1 pound

Pork chops, thin-cut, boneless, 1 pound

Steak, rib-eye or sirloin, boneless, 1 pound

🕐 *Buy thinly sliced flank steak instead of a whole flank steak. You also can ask your butcher to slice a whole flank steak for you!*

Eggs and Dairy

Eggs, large, 20

Brie, 8 ounces

Butter, unsalted, 5 tablespoons

Goat cheese, 3 ounces

🥛 *Brie is made from either cow's milk or goat's milk. Pick a goat's milk Brie if you're avoiding cow's milk dairy but are okay with other types of animal dairy. If neither type works for you, look for cream cheese made with almond milk.*

Substitute ½ cup of ghee for the stick of butter in the Everything Baked Chicken (page 62).

Special Equipment

Bamboo or metal skewers

Produce

Asparagus, 8 ounces

Bird's eye chili peppers, 5

Broccoli florets, 2 (12-ounce) bags

Cauliflower florets, 1 (12-ounce) bag

Garlic, 15 cloves (about 1½ bulbs)

Ginger, 1 (1-inch) piece

Green beans, 1 (12-ounce) package

Lemon, 1

Onions, yellow, 1 small, 1 medium

Parsley, Italian or curly, 2 bunches

Shallots, 5

Spaghetti squash, 2 medium (1 pound each)

Tomatoes, assorted cherry and grape, 2 (10-ounce) packages

Yellow squash, 1 large (about 8 ounces)

Zucchini, 1 large (about 8 ounces)

🕐 *Swap presliced zucchini and yellow squash for the 1 large zucchini and 2 medium yellow squash.*

Swap 4 ounces of premade chimichurri for the parsley, 2 cloves of the garlic, and the olive oil.

🔄 *Bird's eye chili peppers (sometimes called Thai chilis) are available at Asian grocery stores or at local farmers markets. If you can't find any, substitute 1 jalapeño pepper for the 5 bird's eye chilis.*

Meal Prep Game Plan

DAYS AHEAD 3

ESTIMATED TIME SPENT: 15 minutes

1. Read and review the week's menu, grocery list, meal plan, and recipes. Print the downloadable PDF for the week from **easyketomealprep.com/week1**.

   If you want to include keto-friendly snacks or treats to your meal plan for the week, add the ingredients you need to the Other Items category of your grocery list. Some ideas for this week are Italian Roll-Ups (page 268), Cocoa-Dusted Almonds (page 282), and Peanut Butter Fat Bombs (page 284).

2. Review the In Your Pantry section of the grocery list and check off any items that you already have on hand. Be sure you have enough of each pantry item for the recipes you will prepare on meal prep day.

3. Review the Prep Time-Savers, Substitutions, and Dairy Options sections of the grocery list.

   You can buy the convenience items suggested to help cut your prep time this week. Cross off the ingredients that each convenience item replaces on the grocery list.

   Mark ingredients that you need to substitute for; also take note of your preferred dairy option and indicate your choice.

4. Check your calendar for family/work/social events in the coming week. Mark any meals when you won't be eating your prepared dishes. Swap these meals with Leftovers or a Free Meal.

DAYS AHEAD 2

ESTIMATED TIME SPENT: 45 minutes

Shop for groceries. Don't forget your printed grocery list (and Pantry Essentials list if you're shopping for both).

DAY AHEAD 1

ESTIMATED TIME SPENT: 1 hour

POWER HOUR PREP

1. Prepare the following components if you decide not to buy premade chimichurri and everything bagel seasoning:

   - Chimichurri (page 72)
   - Spiced Vinegar (page 74)
   - 5-Ingredient Everything Seasoning (page 75)

2. Marinate the beef for Will's Favorite Beef Tapa (page 56).

3. Prep the aromatics and vegetables.

   Store each aromatic separately in a zip-top plastic bag or airtight glass container in the refrigerator. You can store the zucchini, yellow squash, and asparagus together in one gallon-sized zip-top plastic bag.

   - Mince 13 cloves of garlic (about ¼ cup plus 1 teaspoon) and slice 2 cloves of garlic.
   - Chop 2 shallots and slice 3 shallots.
   - Chop ½ small onion and cut 1 medium onion into 8 wedges.
   - Peel and grate 1 inch of ginger (about ½ tablespoon).
   - Slice the zucchini into 1-inch half-moons.
   - Slice the yellow squash into 1-inch half-moons.
   - Trim the asparagus and cut the spears in half lengthwise.

Cook Once a Week

For your first week of meal prepping, you can cook one item on the stove and another item in the oven at the same time. If you're comfortable cooking more than one item on the stove at a time, feel free to do so.

> *Cool each cooked dish for 10 to 15 minutes before transferring to the containers specified in the* 🗊 *Refrigerate This section of the recipes.*

MEAL PREP DAY

1	Arrange two racks toward the middle of the oven and preheat the oven to 375°F. Cook the sausage and broccoli for the Italian Casserole (page 54) on the stove and then bake the casserole on the bottom rack in the oven.
2	Prepare the Everything Baked Chicken (page 62). Place it on the top rack to bake at the same time as the casserole.
3	Cook the Easy Peasy Hard-Boiled Eggs (page 52) on the stove.
4	While the eggs are cooking, simmer the Weeknight Bolognese (page 64) low and slow on the stove. Remove the eggs from the boiling water and place them in an ice bath immediately.
5	Cook Will's Favorite Beef Tapa (page 56) on the stove. Both the Italian Casserole and Everything Baked Chicken should be done at this point. Remove them from the oven.
6	Prepare the squash for the Spaghetti Squash Noodles (page 68) and bake them in the oven.
7	Prepare and cook the Chimichurri Pork Chops (page 58) on the stove.
8	Cook the Blistered Green Beans (page 66) on the stove.
9	Prepare the Sheet Pan Veggies (page 70) and set aside. The spaghetti squash should be cooked at this point. Remove the dish from the oven and increase the oven temperature to 425°F. Place the Sheet Pan Veggies on the top rack in the oven.
10	Prepare the Sheet Pan Beef and Veggie Kabobs (page 60) and set aside. Once the Sheet Pan Veggies are cooked, remove the pan from the oven and place the Sheet Pan Beef and Veggie Kabobs on the top rack to cook.
11	Prepare the Goat Cheese and Salmon Spread (page 73). Refrigerate it immediately.

Cook Twice a Week

MEAL PREP DAY 1: START OF THE WEEK

1	Preheat the oven to 375°F. Prepare the Everything Baked Chicken (page 62) and bake it in the oven.
2	Cook the Easy Peasy Hard-Boiled Eggs (page 52) on the stove.
3	While the eggs are cooking, cook Will's Favorite Beef Tapa (page 56) on the stove. Remove the eggs from the boiling water and place them in an ice bath immediately. The Everything Baked Chicken should be done at this point. Remove it from the oven and increase the oven temperature to 425°F.
4	Prepare the Sheet Pan Veggies (page 70) and bake them in the oven.
5	Prepare and cook the Blistered Green Beans (page 66) on the stove.
6	Prepare the Sheet Pan Beef and Veggie Kabobs (page 60). The Sheet Pan Veggies should be done at this point. Remove the pan from the oven and place the Sheet Pan Beef and Veggie Kabobs in the oven to cook.
7	Prepare the Goat Cheese and Salmon Spread (page 73). Refrigerate it immediately.

MEAL PREP DAY 2: MIDWEEK

1	Preheat the oven to 375°F. Cook the sausage and broccoli for the Italian Casserole (page 54) on the stove and then bake the casserole in the oven.
2	Simmer the Weeknight Bolognese (page 64) low and slow on the stove.
3	Prepare and cook the Chimichurri Pork Chops (page 58) on the stove.
4	Prepare the squash for the Spaghetti Squash Noodles (page 68) and bake them in the oven.

My Week 1 Meal Prep Notes

Easy Peasy Hard-Boiled Eggs

SERVES 6 · **PREP TIME:** 1 minute · **COOK TIME:** 8 minutes

Take the guesswork out of preparing perfectly cooked hard-boiled eggs every time by following my foolproof technique, which produces a soft and creamy yolk. Prepare the ice bath while the eggs are cooking so you can cool the eggs immediately when the timer goes off.

12 large eggs

4 cups ice

4 cups cold water

1. Keep the eggs in the refrigerator until you're ready to cook them.

2. Fill a medium-sized saucepan with tap water and bring to a boil over medium-high heat.

3. Remove the eggs from the refrigerator and use a slotted spoon to carefully lower the eggs one by one into the boiling water.

4. Set a timer and let the eggs cook uncovered for 8 minutes.

5. While the eggs cook, fill a large bowl with the ice and cold water to create an ice bath for the eggs.

6. After 8 minutes, use a slotted spoon to transfer the eggs one by one to the ice bath. Soaking the eggs in the ice bath cools them immediately so they don't cook further.

7. Let the eggs sit in the ice bath for 5 to 8 minutes, until cold.

Peel the cooled hard-boiled eggs before transferring them to a glass container. Cover and store in the refrigerator for up to 1 week.

Approximate macros per serving: ————
Calories: **143** · Fat: **10g** · Protein: **13g** · Net Carbs: **1g** · Fiber: **0g**

Italian Casserole

SERVES 4 • **PREP TIME:** 5 minutes • **COOK TIME:** 38 minutes

This breakfast casserole has a good amount of meat and vegetables, making it a filling meal. The spices from the Italian sausage flavor the eggs and broccoli, while the Brie adds creaminess and a hint of sweetness to each bite. If you're feeling indulgent, layer a couple of extra slices of Brie on top!

1 pound raw Italian sausage links, casings removed

2 cups fresh broccoli florets, roughly chopped

8 large eggs

½ cup full-fat coconut milk

½ teaspoon sea salt

½ teaspoon black pepper

3 ounces Brie, sliced

1. Preheat the oven to 375°F.

2. Heat a large cast-iron pan over medium-high heat.

3. Put the sausage in the pan and cook, crumbling the meat with a wooden spoon as it cooks, until browned and no longer pink, about 3 minutes.

4. Mix in the broccoli florets and sauté for 5 minutes.

5. Crack the eggs into a large bowl. Pour in the coconut milk and season with the salt and pepper. Whisk until frothy.

6. Transfer the cooked sausage and broccoli to an 11 by 7-inch rectangular baking dish. Pour the egg mixture on top and stir to mix well.

7. Arrange the sliced Brie on top. Bake for 25 to 30 minutes, until the middle of the casserole is firm and the cheese is melted.

Brie usually is made with cow's milk, but if you're looking for a different dairy option, there are brands of goat's milk Brie that have the same great creamy texture. You won't be able to tell the difference between the two! If animal dairy doesn't agree with you, an almond milk-based cream cheese is a tasty, creamy swap for Brie.

Slice the casserole into 8 pieces and cover the top of the baking dish tightly with a sheet of foil. Store in the refrigerator for up to 5 days.

Jenny's tips

Opening a can of coconut milk? Save the unused portion for future use by transferring it to a zip-top freezer bag and storing it in the freezer for up to a month.

Store the extra broccoli in the refrigerator to sauté or blanch later in the week to have an extra fresh side with any meal.

Approximate macros per serving:
Calories: **689** • Fat: **58g** • Protein: **34g** • Net Carbs: **6g** • Fiber: **0g**

Will's Favorite Beef Tapa

Short on marinating time? Marinate the steak first thing in the morning if you're cooking it at night or marinate it at least an hour before cooking.

Transfer the Beef Tapa to a glass container, cover, and store in the refrigerator for up to 1 week.

Transfer the Beef Tapa to a zip-top freezer bag and flatten to remove the excess air before sealing. Store in the freezer for up to 2 months.

Move the bag of frozen Beef Tapa to the refrigerator and let it thaw overnight. Reheat in a skillet over medium-high heat for 2 to 3 minutes.

SERVES 4 · **PREP TIME:** 10 minutes, plus time to marinate overnight
COOK TIME: 15 minutes

This is a family-friendly recipe that you'll want to make again and again—just ask Will! I can't even count the number of times Will has made this recipe, so I dubbed it his favorite. At one point, he was making it every week to share with his son, Diego, and they never got tired of eating it. Buying sliced or shaved steak reduces the prep time from 10 to 2 minutes. You just throw the marinade ingredients in a bag with the beef and put it in the fridge overnight.

1 pound beef flank steak, thinly sliced

¼ cup coconut aminos

3 cloves garlic, minced (about 1 tablespoon)

1 teaspoon fish sauce

½ teaspoon black pepper

¼ teaspoon sea salt

2 tablespoons avocado oil, for frying

1. Place the sliced steak in a zip-top plastic bag.

2. Combine the coconut aminos, garlic, fish sauce, pepper, and salt in a small bowl. Pour the marinade over the beef. Seal the bag and press gently to remove as much air as possible. Place it on the countertop and massage to fully coat the beef with the marinade. Refrigerate overnight.

3. Heat the avocado oil in a cast-iron pan or skillet over medium-high heat.

4. Working in 3 or 4 batches to avoid crowding the pan, place the steak slices in the pan, making sure the ends don't overlap. Pan-fry for 2 minutes. Flip and fry for another 2 minutes.

Approximate macros per serving: ———————
Calories: **273** · Fat: **14g** · Protein: **25g** · Net Carbs: **7g** · Fiber: **0g**

Chimichurri Pork Chops

SERVES 4 • **PREP TIME:** 5 minutes • **COOK TIME:** 3½ minutes

Ever had a recipe take less than 10 minutes to prepare and cook? If not, then these Chimichurri Pork Chops are what you're looking for! The fried chops with a golden-brown crust topped with a dollop of fresh, homemade chimichurri will be a hit with the entire family.

Transfer the pork chops to a glass container, cover, and store in the refrigerator for up to 5 days.

Skip the step where you drizzle the chimichurri over the pork chops. Wrap each pork chop tightly with foil. Place the wrapped chops in a zip-top freezer bag and store in the freezer for up to 2 months. Freeze the chimichurri separately (see the freezing instructions on page 72).

Move the bag of frozen pork chops to the refrigerator and let it thaw overnight. Unwrap each pork chop and reheat it in a skillet over medium heat for 2 minutes.

4 thin-cut boneless pork chops (1 pound)

1 teaspoon sea salt

½ teaspoon black pepper

½ teaspoon garlic powder

½ teaspoon paprika

2 tablespoons avocado oil

½ cup Chimichurri (page 72)

1. Place the pork chops on a plate and pat dry with paper towels. Remove as much excess liquid as possible to help the pork chops develop a nice brown crust as they cook.

2. In a small bowl, combine the salt, pepper, garlic powder, and paprika. Pour the avocado oil into a large cast-iron pan or skillet over medium-high heat.

3. Sprinkle both sides of the pork chops with the prepared seasoning.

4. When the oil is hot, place the pork chops in the pan and fry for 2 minutes. Flip and fry the second side for 1½ minutes.

5. Drizzle the chimichurri over the pork chops. (If you don't plan to refrigerate all four chops to eat in the coming week, skip this step and refer to the freezing instructions on the left.)

Jenny's tips

Thin-cut chops (about ¼-inch thickness) cook quickly, and you easily can overcook them. To prevent them from drying out, make sure you don't cook each side longer than 2 minutes.

If you're cooking thicker pork chops (about ¾-inch thickness), cook each side for an additional 2 minutes.

Approximate macros per serving: —————————
Calories: **348** • Fat: **49g** • Protein: **33g** • Net Carbs: **4g** • Fiber: **2g**

Sheet Pan Beef and Veggie Kabobs

SERVES 4 • **PREP TIME:** 10 minutes • **COOK TIME:** 27 minutes

Cooking marinated beef and vegetable kabobs on a sheet pan in the oven is a wonderful alternative to firing up the grill because you don't need to keep a close eye on them. Using just one pan to cook everything makes cleanup a breeze!

Remove the meat and vegetables from the skewers and transfer to a glass container. Cover and store in the refrigerator for up to 5 days.

Only the beef kabobs are freezer-friendly. Transfer the meat pieces to a zip-top plastic bag and remove as much air as possible. Store in the freezer for up to 2 months.

Transfer the bag of frozen meat to the refrigerator and let it thaw overnight. Reheat the meat in a skillet over medium-high heat for 2 minutes.

FOR THE MARINADE:

½ cup coconut aminos

2 shallots, chopped

1 (1-inch) piece ginger, peeled and grated (about 1 tablespoon)

2 cloves garlic, minced (about 2 teaspoons)

½ teaspoon red pepper flakes

1 pound boneless rib-eye or sirloin steak, cut into 1-inch pieces

1 medium onion, cut into 8 wedges

1 (10-ounce) package cherry tomatoes

1 large zucchini (about 8 ounces), sliced into 1-inch-thick half-moons

Special equipment:
8 bamboo or metal skewers (see Tip)

jenny's tip

If you're using bamboo skewers, fill a rimmed baking sheet with water and soak the skewers for 10 minutes. This will prevent the bamboo from burning in the oven.

1. Preheat the oven to 425°F.

2. Place all the marinade ingredients in a large bowl and mix well.

3. Place the steak in the bowl and toss to coat it with the marinade. Let sit for 5 minutes.

4. Skewer the beef and place it on a rimmed baking sheet.

5. Place the onion, cherry tomatoes, and zucchini in the bowl with the leftover meat marinade. Toss to mix well.

6. Skewer the vegetables and arrange them on the rimmed baking sheet with the skewered beef.

7. Bake for 25 minutes.

8. Turn the oven to broil and broil the kabobs for 2 minutes, until the beef and veggies have a nice brown crust.

Approximate macros per serving:
Calories: **340** • Fat: **21g** • Protein: **23g** • Net Carbs: **11g** • Fiber: **1g**

Everything Baked Chicken

SERVES 4 • **PREP TIME:** 5 minutes • **COOK TIME:** 21 minutes

I usually season chicken with spices and then pan-fry it on the stove, but sometimes I just want to throw a few ingredients together and pop it in the oven to cook. If you were a fan of everything bagels in your pre-keto days, you'll be pleased to hear that adding everything seasoning to chicken tastes just as good!

1 pound boneless, skinless chicken thighs

¼ cup (½ stick) unsalted butter, sliced

5 ounces Brie, sliced

2 tablespoons 5-Ingredient Everything Seasoning (page 75)

1. Preheat the oven to 375°F.

2. Place the chicken thighs flat on a chopping board. Arrange a slice of butter and a slice of Brie on top of each thigh, then roll the chicken so the Brie is stuffed in the middle.

3. Transfer the stuffed chicken to an 11 by 7-inch baking dish with the seam side down. Evenly distribute the remaining slices of butter and Brie on top.

4. Sprinkle the 5-Ingredient Everything Seasoning on top of the chicken.

5. Bake for 20 minutes, until the juices run clear. Turn the oven to broil and broil the chicken for 1 minute so the tops turn golden brown. Keep an eye on the chicken so the seasoning doesn't burn!

Look for goat's milk Brie as an alternative to cow's milk Brie. If animal dairy doesn't agree with you, an almond milk–based cream cheese is a tasty, creamy swap for Brie.

You can use ghee instead of butter for an equally creamy dish.

Cut each stuffed chicken thigh into strips and transfer to a glass container. Cover and store in the refrigerator for up to 5 days.

Do not cut the chicken. Transfer the stuffed chicken thighs to a zip-top freezer bag and remove as much air as possible. Store in the freezer for up to 1 month.

Fill a large bowl with cold water and submerge the bag of frozen chicken. Place it in the fridge for an hour, replacing the water after 30 minutes. Reheat the chicken in the toaster oven for 5 minutes at 375°F or in a skillet over medium-high heat for 3 minutes. Cut into strips before serving.

Approximate macros per serving:
Calories: **245** • Fat: **14g** • Protein: **27g** • Net Carbs: **1g** • Fiber: **0g**

Weeknight Bolognese

I've been making this recipe for as long as I can remember. I have a popular creamy version on my blog, but I always default to this simpler version when I meal prep. Two things make this dish taste like it's been simmering all day regardless of what kind of jarred sauce you use: grass-fed beef and lots of aromatics. Breaking down the beef into small pieces creates a chunky, meaty sauce that screams comfort food!

1 tablespoon ghee

½ small onion, chopped

4 cloves garlic, minced (about 4 teaspoons)

1 pound ground beef

1 (25½-ounce) jar spaghetti or marinara sauce

1. Melt the ghee in a medium saucepan over medium-high heat.

2. Place the onion and garlic in the saucepan and sauté for 1 minute, until fragrant.

3. Add the ground beef and sauté until browned, about 5 minutes.

4. Pour the entire jar of sauce on top of the meat. Stir and bring to a boil.

5. Reduce the heat to low and cover. Let simmer for 25 minutes, stirring halfway through cooking.

Transfer the sauce to two 1-quart wide-mouth mason jars. Cover and store in the refrigerator for up to 5 days.

Transfer the sauce to two 1-quart wide-mouth mason jars, leaving an inch of space at the top to give the sauce room to expand as it freezes. Cover and store in the freezer for up to 2 months.

Transfer the jars of sauce to the refrigerator and let them thaw overnight. Heat the sauce in a medium saucepan over medium-high heat until it begins to simmer.

Jenny's tips

To get every last bit of sauce out of the jar, put ¼ cup of water in the jar, replace the lid, and shake well before pouring it into the pot.

Use an immersion blender to quickly break down the chunks of ground beef after pouring in the sauce.

Approximate macros per serving: ———————
Calories: **301** • Fat: **18g** • Protein: **25g** • Net Carbs: **8g** • Fiber: **2g**

Blistered Green Beans

SERVES 4 · **PREP TIME:** 10 minutes · **COOK TIME:** 11 minutes

Cooking the green beans on high heat browns them nicely and gives them a smokiness that is complemented by the fried shallots and a pat of melted butter.

Buy trimmed, ready-to-cook green beans to save 8 minutes of prep time.

Transfer the green beans to a glass container. Cover and store in the refrigerator for up to 1 week.

1 tablespoon avocado oil

1 (12-ounce) package green beans

2 shallots, thinly sliced

1 tablespoon unsalted butter

1. Heat the avocado oil in a large skillet over medium-high heat.

2. Place the green beans in the pan and sauté for 1 minute. Cover and let the beans cook for 5 to 8 minutes, until they're tender and slightly browned but still have a nice crunch to them.

3. Add the shallots and stir-fry for 2 minutes, until softened.

4. Turn off the heat and place the butter on top of the hot green beans to melt. Mix well to distribute the melted butter evenly.

Approximate macros per serving: —
Calories: **97** · Fat: **7g** · Protein: **2g** · Net Carbs: **6g** · Fiber: **3g**

Spaghetti Squash Noodles

Line the bottom of a glass container with paper towels and transfer the spaghetti squash noodles to the container. The paper towels will absorb the extra liquid to prevent the noodles from getting soggy. Cover and store in the refrigerator for up to 5 days.

jenny's tips

Each roasted spaghetti squash produces about 2 cups of noodles.

Want longer noodle strands? Cut the spaghetti squash in half crosswise instead of cutting it lengthwise.

SERVES 4 • **PREP TIME:** 2 minutes • **COOK TIME:** 35 minutes

My noodle of choice to pair with the Weeknight Bolognese (page 64) has always been these spaghetti squash noodles. The squash roasts nicely in the oven and shreds easily with a fork. It maintains a firm noodlelike texture and absorbs meat sauce like regular pasta noodles do.

2 medium spaghetti squash (about 1 pound each)

1 tablespoon avocado oil

1. Preheat the oven to 375°F.
2. Slice the spaghetti squash in half lengthwise and use a spoon to remove the seeds and stringy flesh.
3. Brush the inside of the squash with the avocado oil and place the halves cut side down on a rimmed baking sheet.
4. Bake for 25 minutes.
5. Flip the squash over and roast for another 10 minutes. It's cooked through when you can easily pierce the flesh with a fork or knife.
6. Let the squash cool for 5 minutes before scraping it lengthwise with a fork to create the noodles.

Approximate macros per serving:
Calories: **46** • Fat: **4g** • Protein: **0g** • Net Carbs: **3g** • Fiber: **1g**

Sheet Pan Veggies

SERVES 4 · **PREP TIME:** 5 minutes · **COOK TIME:** 20 minutes

Transfer the cauliflower and broccoli to a glass container and put the yellow squash and asparagus in another container. Cover and store in the refrigerator for up to 5 days.

Roasting vegetables in the oven on high heat ensures that they brown without turning soggy. Classic seasoning—such as salt, pepper, paprika, and garlic powder—makes these veggies versatile enough to be paired with any main dish.

1 (12-ounce) bag fresh cauliflower florets

1 (12-ounce) bag fresh broccoli florets

1 large yellow squash (about 8 ounces), sliced into 1-inch half-moons

8 ounces asparagus, woody ends removed, sliced in half lengthwise

1 tablespoon avocado oil, divided

1 teaspoon garlic powder

½ teaspoon sea salt

½ teaspoon black pepper

½ teaspoon paprika

1. Preheat the oven to 425°F.

2. Place the cauliflower and broccoli in a large bowl.

3. Drizzle the vegetables with ½ tablespoon of the avocado oil and toss to combine.

4. Mix the garlic powder, salt, pepper, and paprika in a small bowl. Sprinkle half of the seasoning mixture on top of the veggies. Mix well to coat the vegetables evenly with the spices.

5. Transfer the cauliflower and broccoli to a rimmed baking sheet and arrange them evenly so none of the pieces overlap.

6. Place the yellow squash and asparagus in the same bowl used for the cauliflower and broccoli.

7. Drizzle with the other ½ tablespoon of the avocado oil and season with the remaining spices.

8. Mix well and transfer to a second rimmed baking sheet.

9. Roast both trays of vegetables together for 20 minutes.

Approximate macros per serving:
Calories: **86** · Fat: **4g** · Protein: **5g** · Net Carbs: **6g** · Fiber: **5g**

Chimichurri

Transfer the chimichurri to an 8-ounce jar and cover tightly. Store in the refrigerator for up to a week.

Transfer the chimichurri to a zip-top freezer bag and remove as much air as possible before sealing it. Store it flat in the freezer for up to 2 months.

Fill a rimmed baking sheet with cold water and place the bag of chimichurri in it. Allow to defrost for 30 minutes.

Jenny's tip

The extra chimichurri would be a great flavor booster for blanched or roasted vegetables and scrambled eggs!

YIELD: 1 cup, 1 tablespoon per serving • **PREP TIME:** 15 minutes
COOK TIME: —

Nothing beats fresh, homemade chimichurri. Nothing! I've been to restaurants that serve chimichurri that tastes more like oil than like herbs and spices, and I can proudly say my version tastes 100 times better. Using a good-quality olive oil, such as Kasandrinos, makes a big difference, so don't skimp on the ingredients for this chimichurri.

2 bunches Italian or curly parsley leaves, stems removed

¼ cup apple cider vinegar

4 cloves garlic, minced (about 4 teaspoons)

2 teaspoons sea salt

1 teaspoon red pepper flakes

½ cup olive oil

1. Place all the ingredients except the olive oil in a food processor.

2. Cover and pulse for 8 seconds. Open and scrape the sides of the food processor.

3. Pour in the olive oil and replace the lid. Pulse for 10 more seconds.

Approximate macros per serving:
Calories: **65** • Fat: **7g** • Protein: **0g** • Net Carbs: **1g** • Fiber: **0g**

Goat Cheese and Salmon Spread

Transfer to a glass container and store in the refrigerator for up to 5 days.

YIELD: 1 cup, ¼ cup per serving • **PREP TIME:** 5 minutes
COOK TIME: —

Goat cheese and salmon? Yes, please! Use this spread as a dip for crudité or to jazz up some Easy Peasy Hard-Boiled Eggs (page 52) to create a protein- and fat-packed meal. The addition of lemon juice and zest gives the spread a punch of freshness.

3 ounces fresh goat cheese, crumbled

1 (6-ounce) can unsalted flaked salmon, drained

1 tablespoon grated lemon zest

Juice of 1 lemon (about 2 tablespoons)

1 teaspoon black pepper

½ teaspoon sea salt

Place all the ingredients in a medium-sized bowl. Mix well to combine.

Approximate macros per serving: ————————————
Calories: **183** • Fat: **9g** • Protein: **6g** • Net Carbs: **1g** • Fiber: **2g**

Spiced Vinegar

 Store the Spiced Vinegar in the pantry for up to 1 month.

YIELD: 1 cup, 2 tablespoons per serving • **PREP TIME:** 5 minutes
COOK TIME: —

One of the most important parts of a Filipino meal is the dipping sauce (sawsawan) that is served with it. I love spicy food, so this Spiced Vinegar (Sukang Maanghang) is a condiment that you'll always find in my kitchen. There are different bottled, ready-to-use brands available at Asian grocery stores, but I prefer to make my own, so it's fresher and free from unnecessary additives.

1 cup apple cider vinegar

5 whole bird's eye chili peppers, 1 pepper sliced in half

2 cloves garlic, thinly sliced

1 shallot, thinly sliced

1 teaspoon fish sauce

1 teaspoon whole black peppercorns

Place all the ingredients in a pint-sized wide-mouth mason jar. Cover and let sit at room temperature for a day to let the flavors blend before you use it.

Jenny's tip

You can substitute 1 jalapeño pepper for all the bird's eye chili peppers. Cut off the stem end and slice the pepper in half lengthwise before placing it in the jar.

Approximate macros per serving:
Calories: **21** • Fat: **1g** • Protein: **1g** • Net Carbs: **3g** • Fiber: **1g**

5-Ingredient Everything Seasoning

 Store the seasoning in the pantry for up to 2 months.

YIELD: ½ cup, 1 tablespoon per serving • **PREP TIME:** 5 minutes
COOK TIME: —

This blend is a great to use as a topping for the Easy Peasy Hard-Boiled Eggs (page 52) and as a seasoning for the Everything Baked Chicken (page 62). Using flaked sea salt makes such a big difference in the flavor!

2 tablespoons sesame seeds

1½ tablespoons flaked sea salt

1½ tablespoons dried minced garlic

1½ tablespoons dried minced onion

1 tablespoon poppy seeds

Place all the ingredients in a pint-sized wide-mouth mason jar. Cover and shake to mix well.

Approximate macros per serving: ————————
Calories: **25** • Fat: **2g** • Protein: **1g** • Net Carbs: **1g** • Fiber: **1g**

Build Your Plate

Easy Peasy Hard-Boiled Eggs, Goat Cheese and Salmon Spread, 5-Ingredient Everything Seasoning, cherry and grape tomatoes with balsamic vinegar

1. Boil 3 cups of water and pour it into a large bowl. Grab 4 hard-boiled eggs from the refrigerator and place them in the hot water for 5 minutes to warm them.

2. Cut the eggs in half and divide them between two plates.

3. Top each egg with 1 tablespoon of Goat Cheese and Salmon Spread (page 73).

4. Sprinkle with 1 tablespoon of 5-Ingredient Everything Seasoning (page 75).

5. Halve the assorted cherry and grape tomatoes and divide them between the two plates.

6. Drizzle 1 tablespoon of balsamic vinegar on the tomatoes and season them with a pinch of salt and pepper.

Italian Casserole

1. Heat two servings of the Italian Casserole (page 54) in the microwave on high for 1 minute or in a lightly oiled preheated skillet over medium-high heat for 2 minutes.

2. Divide the servings between two plates.

Will's Favorite Beef Tapa, Spiced Vinegar, Sheet Pan Veggies (cauliflower and broccoli)

1. Heat two servings of the Beef Tapa (page 56) and the cauliflower and broccoli from the Sheet Pan Veggies (page 70) in the toaster oven at 375°F for 3 minutes or in a preheated skillet over medium-high heat for 3 minutes.

2. Divide the beef and vegetables between two plates and serve each with 2 tablespoons of Spiced Vinegar (page 74) on the side for dipping.

Everything Baked Chicken, Blistered Green Beans

1. Heat two servings of the Everything Baked Chicken (page 62) and Blistered Green Beans (page 66) in the microwave on high for 1 minute or in a lightly oiled preheated skillet over medium-high heat for 2 minutes.

2. Divide the chicken and green beans between two plates.

Chimichurri Pork Chops, Chimichurri, Sheet Pan Veggies (yellow squash and asparagus)

1. Heat two of the Chimichurri Pork Chops (page 58) and the yellow squash and asparagus from the Sheet Pan Veggies (page 70) in a lightly oiled preheated skillet over medium-high heat for 2 minutes.

2. Divide the pork chops and veggies between two plates.

3. Drizzle 1 tablespoon of the Chimichurri on top of each pork chop.

Sheet Pan Beef and Veggie Kabobs

1. Heat two servings of the beef and vegetables from the Sheet Pan Beef and Veggie Kabobs (page 60) in the microwave on high for 1 minute or in the toaster oven at 375°F for 3 minutes.

2. Divide the beef and vegetables between two plates.

Weeknight Bolognese, Spaghetti Squash Noodles

1. Place 1 cup of the Spaghetti Squash Noodles (page 68) in each of two bowls, then place one serving of the Weeknight Bolognese (page 64) on top of each portion of noodles.

2. Microwave on high for 2 minutes.

WEEK 2

Getting Started

Now that you've completed week 1, you should have a good feel for how meal prepping works. The recipes for week 2 are still easy to make, and you cook most dishes with one pan. This week, you continue to use two cooking methods, stove and oven, to get yourself used to preparing multiple dishes at the same time.

Print the downloadable Week 2 PDF from **easyketomealprep.com/week2.**

What's on the Menu

If you need to adjust the quantities of the recipes for your needs, see the table on page 33 in the "What's on the Menu" section in the Introduction for more information.

MAIN DISHES

Loaded Hamburger Hash

COOKING METHOD:

PREP TIME: 10 minutes

COOK TIME: 14 minutes

SERVES 6

Savory Breakfast Plate

COOKING METHOD:

PREP TIME: 5 minutes

COOK TIME: 8 minutes

SERVES 4

Turkey Mushroom Sauté

COOKING METHOD:

PREP TIME: 5 minutes

COOK TIME: 13 minutes

SERVES 4

Crispy Carnitas

COOKING METHOD:

PREP TIME: 10 minutes

COOK TIME: 95 minutes

SERVES 4

Pesto Meatballs

COOKING METHOD:

PREP TIME: 10 minutes

COOK TIME: 20 minutes

SERVES 8

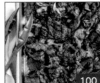

Carne Asada

COOKING METHOD:

PREP TIME: 10 minutes

COOK TIME: 28 minutes

SERVES 8

Chicken Adobo

COOKING METHOD:

PREP TIME: 15 minutes

COOK TIME: 35 minutes

SERVES 8

save half for later

The Pesto Meatballs (page 98), Carne Asada (page 100), and Chicken Adobo (page 102) recipes make enough so you can freeze half of each dish. Refer to the ❄ *Freeze This section in each recipe for specific freezing instructions.*

The Turkey Mushroom Sauté (page 94) and Crispy Carnitas (page 96) also are freezer-friendly recipes.

jenny's meal prep tip

Pack and Label Prepped Food

Pack each main dish, side, and garnish separately so food lasts longer in the fridge. Label each container with a sticky note so you or your family aren't wondering what's inside. Putting a plate together will be a breeze because the labels help you identify exactly what to grab rather than having to look at each package one by one!

SIDES

Blanched Bok Choy

COOKING METHOD: 〰️
PREP TIME: 1 minute
COOK TIME: 3 minutes
SERVES 4

Zesty Slaw

COOKING METHOD: —
PREP TIME: 15 minutes
COOK TIME: —
SERVES 4

Balsamic Roasted Tomatoes

COOKING METHOD: 🔲
PREP TIME: 5 minutes
COOK TIME: 27 minutes
SERVES 4

Turmeric Garlic Cauliflower Rice

COOKING METHOD: 〰️
PREP TIME: 10 minutes
COOK TIME: 10 minutes
SERVES 4

Roasted Sweet Peppers and Onions

COOKING METHOD: 🔲
PREP TIME: 10 minutes
COOK TIME: 35 minutes
SERVES 4

Zucchini Noodles

COOKING METHOD: 〰️
PREP TIME: 25 minutes
COOK TIME: 1 minute
SERVES 4

CONDIMENTS AND GARNISHES

Chili Oil

COOKING METHOD: 〰️
PREP TIME: 2 minutes
COOK TIME: 1 minute
YIELD: ½ cup

Pico de Gallo

COOKING METHOD: —
PREP TIME: 15 minutes
COOK TIME: —
YIELD: 2 cups

Sliced avocados

Arugula

Limes

Shaved Parmesan cheese

Meal Plan

Cook Once a Week

DAY	BREAKFAST		LUNCH		DINNER	
1	Savory Breakfast Plate		Turkey Mushroom Sauté, Blanched Bok Choy, Chili Oil		Pesto Meatballs, Zucchini Noodles, Parmesan cheese	
2	Loaded Hamburger Hash with sliced avocado		Pesto Meatballs, Zucchini Noodles, Parmesan cheese		Crispy Carnitas, Zesty Slaw, Pico de Gallo	
3	Loaded Hamburger Hash with sliced avocado		Turkey Mushroom Sauté, Blanched Bok Choy, Chili Oil		Carne Asada, Roasted Sweet Peppers and Onion, Pico de Gallo, limes	
4	Savory Breakfast Plate		Chicken Adobo, Turmeric Garlic Cauliflower Rice		Crispy Carnitas, Zesty Slaw, Pico de Gallo	
5	Loaded Hamburger Hash with sliced avocado		Carne Asada, Roasted Sweet Peppers and Onion, Pico de Gallo, limes		Chicken Adobo, Turmeric Garlic Cauliflower Rice	
6	Free Meal		Leftovers		Leftovers	
7	Free Meal		Leftovers		Leftovers	

Cook Twice a Week

DAY	BREAKFAST	LUNCH	DINNER
1	Loaded Hamburger Hash with sliced avocado	Turkey Mushroom Sauté, Blanched Bok Choy, Chili Oil	Pesto Meatballs, Zucchini Noodles, Parmesan cheese
2	Loaded Hamburger Hash with sliced avocado	Carne Asada, Roasted Sweet Peppers and Onion, Pico de Gallo, limes	Turkey Mushroom Sauté, Blanched Bok Choy, Chili Oil
3	Loaded Hamburger Hash with sliced avocado	Pesto Meatballs, Zucchini Noodles, Parmesan cheese	Chicken Adobo, Turmeric Garlic Cauliflower Rice
4	Savory Breakfast Plate	Carne Asada, Roasted Sweet Peppers and Onion, Pico de Gallo, limes	Crispy Carnitas, Zesty Slaw, Pico de Gallo
5	Savory Breakfast Plate	Crispy Carnitas, Zesty Slaw, Pico de Gallo	Chicken Adobo, Turmeric Garlic Cauliflower Rice
6	Free Meal	Leftovers	Leftovers
7	Free Meal	Leftovers	Leftovers

Grocery List

In Your Pantry

Apple cider vinegar, ¾ cup

Balsamic vinegar, 2 tablespoons

Bay leaves, 5

Black pepper, 2 tablespoons plus ¾ teaspoon

Coconut aminos, 1½ cups plus 2 tablespoons

Coconut milk, full-fat, 1 (13½-ounce) can

Fish sauce, 2 teaspoons

Garlic powder, 1 tablespoon plus ½ teaspoon

Ghee, ¼ cup plus 1 tablespoon

Ground cumin, ¼ teaspoon

Ground dried oregano, 1 teaspoon

Olive oil, 1¾ cups

Olive oil spray

Onion powder, ½ teaspoon

Paprika, ⅛ teaspoon

Red pepper flakes, 1 tablespoon plus ½ teaspoon

Sea salt, ⅓ cup

Toasted sesame oil, 2½ tablespoons

*Do you need to replenish any pantry items this week? Add them to your grocery list. You can print the downloadable list from **easyketomealprep.com/pantry** to take with you to the grocery store. Check off all the items under the In Your Pantry category because these are already on the Pantry Essentials list.*

Frozen Items

Riced cauliflower, 2 (12-ounce) bags

Eggs and Dairy

Parmesan cheese, shaved, 1 cup (about 2 ounces)

Substitute 1 cup of crumbled fresh goat cheese, sheep's milk feta, or almond milk ricotta for the shaved Parmesan cheese.

Condiments and Spices

Turmeric powder, 2 teaspoons

Meat and Seafood

Beef, skirt steak, 2 pounds

Beef, ground, 2½ pounds

Chicken, 1 whole (about 4½ pounds)

Hot dogs, beef, 1 (10-ounce) package (includes 4 hot dogs)

Pork, ground, 1 pound

Pork butt or pork shoulder, boneless, 2 pounds

Turkey, ground, 1 pound

Swap skirt steak for Carne Asada–style chuck roast. Some grocery stores will thinly slice chuck roast for free.

Swap 4 pounds of drumsticks for the whole chicken. You can also ask your butcher to cut up a whole chicken, so you won't have to do that at home.

Produce

Baby arugula, 1 (8-ounce) bag

Baby bok choy, 1 pound

Basil, 1 pack (about 4 ounces)

Bird's eye chili peppers, 4 (optional)

Cabbage, green, ½ head

Cabbage, red, ½ head

Cilantro, 2 bunches

Garlic, 27 cloves (about 3 bulbs)

Ginger, 1 (4-inch) piece

Green onions, 1 bunch

Hass avocados, 5 medium

Jalapeño peppers, 4

Kale, 1 bunch (about 1 pound)

Lemons, 3

Limes, 5

Mini sweet peppers (any color), 1 pound

Mushrooms, white or cremini (baby bella), sliced, 2 packages (about 8 ounces each)

Navel oranges, 2

Onions, yellow, 3 small, 1 medium

Tomatoes, cherry, 3 (10-ounce) packages

Tomatoes, Roma, 3

Zucchini, 8 large (about 4 pounds)

Swap 2 (12-ounce) bags of shredded coleslaw for the ½ head of green cabbage and the ½ head of red cabbage.

Swap 4 pounds of ready-to-use spiral-sliced zucchini noodles for the 8 large zucchini.

Swap 8 ounces of jarred pesto for the package of basil, ½ cup of the Parmesan cheese, and 4 cloves of the garlic.

Swap 16 ounces of premade salsa for the Roma tomatoes, ½ of a small yellow onion, 1 jalapeño pepper, and 1 bunch of the cilantro.

Meal Prep Game Plan

ESTIMATED TIME SPENT: 15 minutes

1. Read and review the week's menu, grocery list, meal plan, and recipes. Print the downloadable PDF for the week.

   If you want to include keto-friendly snacks or treats to your meal plan for the week, add the ingredients you need to the Other Items category of your grocery list. Some ideas for this week are Deviled Eggs (page 258), No-Bake Blueberry Cheesecake Cups (page 278), and Iced Matcha (page 290).

2. Review the In Your Pantry section of the grocery list and check off any items that you already have on hand. Be sure you have enough of each pantry item for the recipes you will prepare on meal prep day.

3. Review the Prep Time-Savers, Substitutions, and Dairy Options sections of the grocery list.

   You can buy the convenience items suggested to help cut your prep time this week. Cross off the ingredients that each convenience item replaces on the grocery list.

   Mark ingredients that you need to substitute for; also take note of your preferred dairy option and indicate your choice.

4. Check your calendar for family/work/social events in the coming week. Mark any meals when you won't be eating your prepared dishes. Swap these meals with Leftovers or a Free Meal.

ESTIMATED TIME SPENT: 45 minutes

Shop for groceries. Don't forget your printed grocery list (and Pantry Essentials list if you're shopping for both).

ESTIMATED TIME SPENT: 1 hour

POWER HOUR PREP

1. Prepare the following components if you decide not to buy premade pesto:

   - Pesto for the Pesto Meatballs (page 98)
   - Chili Oil (page 116)

2. Prep the aromatics and vegetables.

   Store each aromatic separately in a zip-top plastic bag or airtight glass container in the refrigerator.

   - Chop 2½ small onions and 1 medium onion.
   - Mince 27 cloves of garlic (about ½ cup plus 1 tablespoon).
   - Peel and grate 3 inches of ginger (about 1½ tablespoons).
   - Peel and slice 1 inch of ginger.
   - Spiral-slice the zucchini.
   - Shred the green and red cabbage.

Cook Once a Week

To maximize your time on meal prep day, follow the suggested order for preparing each dish. This week's prep involves cooking multiple items at the same time in the oven and on the stove.

Cool each cooked dish for 10 to 15 minutes before transferring to the containers specified in the 🄱 *Refrigerate This section of the recipes.*

MEAL PREP DAY

1	Arrange two racks toward the middle of the oven and preheat the oven to 375°F. Prepare the Balsamic Roasted Tomatoes (page 108) to the point they're ready for the oven. Prepare the Roasted Sweet Peppers and Onions (page 112) as well. Place the Balsamic Roasted Tomatoes on the top rack and the Roasted Sweet Peppers and Onions on the bottom rack in the oven to bake at the same time.
2	While the vegetables are in the oven, cook the Chicken Adobo (page 102) on the stove.
3	Halfway through the cook time for the Roasted Sweet Peppers and Onions, flip over the peppers and onions. Remove the Balsamic Roasted Tomatoes from the oven when the skins are soft and shriveled. Set the tomatoes aside until the Roasted Sweet Peppers and Onions are done and you can remove them from the oven. Switch the oven to a higher temperature, and place the Balsamic Roasted Tomatoes back in the oven on the top rack to broil for 2 minutes. Remove the tomatoes from the oven when they have a caramelized crust. Turn the oven back down to 375°F.
4	While the Chicken Adobo simmers, cook the Loaded Hamburger Hash (page 90) on the stove.
5	The Chicken Adobo should be done a few minutes before the Loaded Hamburger Hash is done. Turn off the heat for the Chicken Adobo and finish cooking the hash.
6	Prepare the Crispy Carnitas (page 96) and bake the pork in the oven at 375°F.
7	While the Crispy Carnitas is baking, cook the Turkey Mushroom Sauté (page 94) on the stove.

8	Once the Turkey Mushroom Sauté is done, cook the Pesto Meatballs (page 98) on the stove. If you prefer the oven method, bake them in the oven at the same time as the Crispy Carnitas because both are baked at 375°F.
9	While the Pesto Meatballs are cooking, grill the Carne Asada (page 100) on the stove.
10	Once the Pesto Meatballs and Carne Asada are done, remove the bags of riced cauliflower from the freezer and thaw at room temperature.
11	Cook the Zucchini Noodles (page 114) on the stove.
12	Pan-fry the hot dogs for the Savory Breakfast Plate (page 92) on the stove.
13	The Crispy Carnitas should be done at this point. Shred the pork with two forks and switch the oven to a high temperature to broil the carnitas. Remove the carnitas from the oven when the edges are crispy.
14	Cook the Turmeric Garlic Cauliflower Rice (page 110) on the stove.
15	Cook the Blanched Bok Choy (page 104) on the stove.
16	Prepare the Zesty Slaw (page 106). Refrigerate immediately.
17	Prepare the Pico de Gallo (page 118). Refrigerate immediately.

MEAL PREP DAY 1: START OF THE WEEK

1	Preheat the oven to 375°F. Bake the Roasted Sweet Peppers and Onions (page 112) in the oven.
2	While the vegetables are in the oven, cook the Loaded Hamburger Hash (page 90) on the stove. Halfway through the cook time for the Roasted Sweet Peppers and Onions, flip over the peppers and onions.
3	Cook the Turkey Mushroom Sauté (page 94) on the stove.
4	Once the Turkey Mushroom Sauté is done, prepare the Pesto Meatballs (page 98) and cook them on the stove or bake them in the oven.
5	While the Pesto Meatballs are cooking or baking, grill the Carne Asada (page 100) on the stove.
6	Cook the Zucchini Noodles (page 114) on the stove.
7	Cook the Blanched Bok Choy (page 104) on the stove.
8	Prepare the Pico de Gallo (page 118). Refrigerate immediately.

MEAL PREP DAY 2: MIDWEEK

1	Preheat the oven to 375°F. Bake the Balsamic Roasted Tomatoes (page 108) in the oven.
2	While the tomatoes are cooking, cook the Chicken Adobo (page 102) on the stove. Remove the bags of riced cauliflower from the freezer and thaw them at room temperature.
3	Pan-fry the hot dogs for the Savory Breakfast Plate (page 92) on the stove.
4	Once the roasted tomatoes are done, bake the Crispy Carnitas (page 96) in the oven at 375°F.
5	Cook the Turmeric Garlic Cauliflower Rice (page 110) on the stove.
6	Prepare the Zesty Slaw (page 106). Refrigerate immediately.
7	The Crispy Carnitas should be done at this point. Shred the pork with two forks and switch the oven to a high temperature to broil the carnitas. Remove the carnitas from the oven when the edges are crispy.

My Week 2 Meal Prep Notes

Loaded Hamburger Hash

SERVES 6 • **PREP TIME:** 10 minutes • **COOK TIME:** 14 minutes

Substitute crumbled fresh goat cheese, sheep's milk feta, or almond milk ricotta for the Parmesan cheese.

Transfer the hash to a glass container, cover, and store in the refrigerator for up to 5 days.

note

Refer to Build Your Plate on page 120 for instructions on how to serve the Loaded Hamburger Hash with the avocados and extra Parmesan.

I'm a big fan of sautéed ground meat because it reheats well but doesn't taste like leftovers. This Loaded Hamburger Hash has a good amount of mushrooms and kale to make it a hearty and filling bowl. A squeeze of lemon juice gives the dish a nice zing, and the shaved Parmesan adds a little nutty flavor.

1½ tablespoons ghee

1 small onion, chopped

4 cloves garlic, minced (about 4 teaspoons)

1½ pounds ground beef

¾ teaspoon sea salt

¾ teaspoon black pepper

8 ounces sliced white or cremini mushrooms

1 bunch kale (about 1 pound), destemmed and chopped into 3-inch pieces

½ cup shaved Parmesan cheese, plus extra for garnish

Juice of 1 lemon (about 2 tablespoons)

1. Heat a large skillet or cast-iron pan over medium-high heat.

2. Put the ghee in the hot skillet and let it melt for a few seconds. Add the onion and garlic and sauté for 2 to 3 minutes, until the onion begins to soften and becomes translucent.

3. Add the ground beef and season it with the salt and pepper. Cook, stirring to crumble the meat, until the beef is no longer pink, about 3 minutes.

4. Add the mushrooms and stir to combine with the ground beef. Cook for 3 to 5 minutes, until the mushrooms are tender.

5. Add the kale and carefully mix it with the ground beef and mushrooms so it doesn't overflow. You may think you have too much kale at first, but it will shrink significantly. Cook until the kale is wilted, 2 to 3 minutes.

   Turn off the heat and add the Parmesan cheese and lemon juice. Stir to combine. The Parmesan cheese will melt slightly to give you nice, cheesy chunks of meat. Garnish with a little bit more Parmesan on top, if desired.

Approximate macros per serving: —————
Calories: **326** • Fat: **23g** • Protein: **19g** • Net Carbs: **10g** • Fiber: **3g**

Savory Breakfast Plate

SERVES 4 · **PREP TIME:** 5 minutes · **COOK TIME:** 8 minutes

Eating keto doesn't have to be complicated, and simple meals for breakfast are always best. This Savory Breakfast Plate was my go-to meal when I first started eating keto. It's a light meal that got me through the morning until lunchtime!

1 tablespoon ghee

4 beef hot dogs (about 2½ ounces each)

1 batch Balsamic Roasted Tomatoes (page 108)

1 (8-ounce) bag baby arugula

2 medium Hass avocados

1. Heat a large cast-iron pan over medium-high heat.

2. Put the ghee in the pan and let it melt for a few seconds. Add the hot dogs and pan-fry for 5 to 8 minutes, until golden brown.

3. Divide the Balsamic Roasted Tomatoes and hot dogs between four plates.

4. Slice two avocados and place ¼ of the slices on each plate. Add a cup of baby arugula to each plate.

Transfer the hot dogs to a glass container, cover, and store in the refrigerator for up to 5 days.

Approximate macros per serving:
Calories: **427** · Fat: **32.5g** · Protein: **13g** · Net Carbs: **8g** · Fiber: **9g**

Turkey Mushroom Sauté

SERVES 4 • **PREP TIME:** 5 minutes • **COOK TIME:** 13 minutes

Before I went keto, my appetizer of choice at Asian restaurants was always the lettuce cups. There's something about ground meat and chunks of mushrooms slathered in a soy and sesame sauce that makes me want to eat more. I created a simpler version of this old-time favorite and used cleaner ingredients that have the same great taste. This recipe also works with ground pork if you prefer it to ground turkey. Drizzling a little bit of Chili Oil (page 116) on the turkey sauté completes this dish.

1½ tablespoons ghee

4 cloves garlic, minced (about 4 teaspoons)

1 (3-inch) piece ginger, peeled and grated (about 1½ tablespoons)

1 pound ground turkey

8 ounces sliced white or cremini mushrooms

¼ cup plus 2 tablespoons coconut aminos

2 teaspoons fish sauce

1 teaspoon black pepper

1½ tablespoons toasted sesame oil

¼ cup chopped green onions, for topping

1. Heat a large cast-iron pan over medium-high heat.

2. Put the ghee in the hot pan and let it melt for a few seconds. Add the garlic and ginger to the pan. Sauté for 1 minute, until the garlic begins to turn golden brown but is not burned.

3. Add the ground turkey and cook for 3 to 4 minutes, using a wooden spoon to break down the turkey chunks into smaller pieces so the meat can be seasoned evenly.

4. Add the mushrooms and stir to combine with the turkey. Season with the coconut aminos, fish sauce, and pepper. Stir for a few more seconds to combine everything, then cook for 5 to 8 minutes, until the turkey is cooked through and the mushrooms are tender.

5. Season with the sesame oil and mix well. Top with the green onions.

Transfer the ground turkey to a glass container, cover, and store in the refrigerator for up to 5 days.

Transfer the ground turkey to a zip-top freezer bag and flatten to remove any excess air before sealing. Store in the freezer for up to 2 months.

Fill a rimmed sheet pan with about 1 inch of cold water. Move the bag of frozen Turkey Mushroom Sauté to the sheet pan and put the pan in the refrigerator for an hour, replacing the water after 30 minutes. Transfer the Turkey Mushroom Sauté to a microwave-safe dish and cook on high for 1 to 2 minutes, or reheat in a skillet over medium-high heat for 2 minutes.

Approximate macros per serving: ————————
Calories: **275** • Fat: **16g** • Protein: **24g** • Net Carbs: **9g** • Fiber: **1g**

Crispy Carnitas

SERVES 4 • **PREP TIME:** 10 minutes • **COOK TIME:** 95 minutes

Transfer the carnitas to a glass container, cover, and store in the refrigerator for up to 1 week.

Transfer the carnitas to a zip-top freezer bag and flatten to remove any excess air before sealing. Store in the freezer for up to 3 months.

Move the bag of frozen carnitas to the refrigerator and let it thaw overnight. Reheat the carnitas in a skillet over medium-high heat for 3 minutes, until it crisps up again.

Jenny's tip

Place the carnitas in a stand mixer fitted with a flat beater attachment. Turn it on medium-low speed for 10 seconds to shred the pork.

My foolproof carnitas has been one of my most popular blog recipes because it's super easy to make. I created this version based on my original and added ingredients to give it a different flavor dimension. A little bit of fresh orange juice brightens it up without adding a ton of sugar (only about 5 grams for the entire recipe), so this is still very much keto!

2 pounds boneless pork butt or shoulder, cut into 2-inch pieces

1 medium onion, chopped (about ¾ cup)

¼ cup freshly squeezed orange juice

4 cloves garlic, minced (about 4 teaspoons)

1½ teaspoons sea salt

1 teaspoon dried ground oregano

1 teaspoon black pepper

¼ teaspoon ground cumin

2 limes, quartered, for serving

1. Preheat the oven to 375°F.

2. Place all the ingredients in a large bowl. Using your hands, mix everything together. Make sure each piece of pork is covered with the spices.

3. Transfer the seasoned pork to a rimmed baking sheet and arrange it evenly in one layer. Move any onion pieces that are on the edge of the baking sheet toward the middle to keep them from burning while cooking.

4. Cover the baking sheet with two overlapping sheets of foil (each about 16 inches long) and tightly crimp it around the edges. Remove any excess foil that would get snagged when you place the pan in the oven. Punch eight random holes in the foil using the tip of a knife.

5. Cook the carnitas for 90 minutes. Rotate the baking sheet at the 45-minute mark to make sure that the carnitas cooks evenly.

6. Remove the carnitas from the oven and let cool for about 5 minutes (so you won't have a lot of steam when you take the foil off).

7. Carefully remove and discard the foil. Shred the carnitas with two forks. The meat will be tender and easy to shred. The onions will be super soft and caramelized. Mix the onions with the carnitas to incorporate all the flavors before broiling.

Approximate macros per serving:
Calories: **635** • Fat: **43g** • Protein: **53g** • Net Carbs: **6g** • Fiber: **1g**

8. Turn the oven to broil. Place the carnitas back in the oven and broil for 3 to 5 minutes, until the edges are crispy. Keep a close eye on the carnitas and take it out as soon as the timer ends so the pork doesn't dry out or burn.

Pesto Meatballs

SERVES 8 • **PREP TIME:** 10 minutes • **COOK TIME:** 20 minutes

Nothing beats the taste of fresh, homemade pesto, and it's hard to resist not eating it by the spoonful. I leave out the nuts to make the dish affordable and easier to bring to a potluck or gathering in case anyone has a nut allergy, but the pesto has a good amount of garlic and Parmesan cheese that creates such a chunky texture, you won't even realize there are no nuts! You can either pan-fry the meatballs on the stove or pop them in the oven to bake. Either way, you'll have perfectly cooked meatballs!

FOR THE PESTO
(makes about 1 cup):

4 ounces fresh basil, stemmed

½ cup shaved Parmesan cheese

½ cup olive oil

4 cloves garlic, minced (about 4 teaspoons)

1 teaspoon sea salt

1 teaspoon black pepper

½ teaspoon red pepper flakes

FOR THE MEATBALLS:

1 pound ground beef

1 pound ground pork

Pesto (from the left), divided

2 teaspoons sea salt

1 teaspoon black pepper

1 tablespoon ghee, for the pan

TO MAKE THE PESTO:

1. Place the basil, Parmesan cheese, olive oil, and garlic in a food processor. Cover and pulse for 10 seconds.

2. Remove the cover and scrape the sides of the bowl. Replace the cover and pulse for another 10 seconds.

3. Remove the blade from the food processor and carefully scrape the excess pesto on the blade back into the bowl. Season with the salt, pepper, and red pepper flakes. Mix well.

4. Divide the pesto equally into 2 small bowls (each bowl should have about ½ cup of pesto). You'll use one portion as a seasoning for the meatballs and the other to toss the cooked meatballs in.

No time to make your own pesto? Buy jarred pesto made with clean ingredients and save about 5 minutes of prep time.

Transfer one portion of the meatballs to a glass container, cover, and store in the refrigerator for up to 5 days.

Transfer the remaining meatballs to a zip-top freezer bag and gently squeeze to remove any excess air before sealing. Store in the freezer for up to 2 months.

Fill a deep bowl with cold water and submerge the bag of frozen meatballs in it; put the bowl in the refrigerator for an hour, replacing the water after 30 minutes. Reheat the meatballs in a skillet over medium heat for 2 minutes.

Approximate macros per serving:
Calories: **400** • Fat: **34g** • Protein: **24g** • Net Carbs: **1g** • Fiber: **0g**

TO MAKE THE MEATBALLS:

1. Place the ground beef, ground pork, one half of the pesto, the salt, and the black pepper in a large bowl. Mix everything together using your hands.

2. Grab a tablespoon's worth (about 1 ounce) of the meatball mixture and form it into a 1½-inch meatball. Repeat until you have 24 meatballs.

TO BAKE THE MEATBALLS:

1. Preheat the oven to 375°F.

2. For easier cleanup, line a rimmed baking sheet with parchment paper.

3. Arrange the meatballs evenly on the prepared baking sheet and bake for 20 minutes, until cooked through. Drizzle the remaining pesto on top of the meatballs and toss to combine.

TO PAN-FRY THE MEATBALLS:

1. Heat a large cast-iron pan over medium heat.

2. Put the ghee in the hot pan and let it melt for a few seconds. Place 12 meatballs in the pan. Space them evenly so the sides don't touch. Pan-fry for 8 to 10 minutes, until all sides are browned and the meatballs are cooked through.

3. Transfer the cooked meatballs to a medium-sized bowl. Pan-fry the remaining meatballs.

4. When the second batch of meatballs is cooked, turn off the heat and return the first batch of meatballs to the pan. Pour the remaining pesto on top and stir until the meatballs are evenly coated.

Carne Asada

SERVES 8 • **PREP TIME:** 10 minutes, plus time to marinate overnight
COOK TIME: 28 minutes

My coworker Leah (who I call my "mama") has graciously shared with me the ingredients of her super-simple Carne Asada recipe. She cooks by taste (a sign of an amazing cook!), so I experimented with the measurements for the marinade until I nailed down the right ratio. I love how the vibrant marinade is slightly sweet and tart thanks to the addition of orange and lemon juice. The green onions add another layer of YUM to the meat once it's cooked and caramelized.

Buy presliced "carne asada-style" chuck roast to save about 8 minutes of prep time. Some butchers and grocery stores offer to slice chuck roast for free!

Transfer one portion of the Carne Asada to a glass container, cover, and store in the refrigerator for up to 1 week.

Transfer the remaining Carne Asada to a zip-top freezer bag and flatten to remove any excess air before sealing. Store in the freezer for up to 3 months.

Move the bag of frozen Carne Asada to the refrigerator and let it thaw overnight. Reheat the Carne Asada in a skillet over medium-high heat for 3 to 4 minutes.

FOR THE MARINADE:

Juice of 1 orange (about ½ cup)

Juice of 2 lemons (about ¼ cup)

1 cup sliced green onions

½ cup coconut aminos

¼ cup olive oil

2 pounds boneless chuck roast or skirt steak, sliced ¼ inch thick

2 ½ teaspoons sea salt

1 teaspoon black pepper

1. In a large bowl, whisk together the ingredients for the marinade.

2. Add the sliced chuck roast or skirt steak and use your hands to evenly distribute the marinade and coat each piece of the meat.

3. Place the meat and the marinade in a gallon-sized zip-top bag. Gently press the bag to remove as much air as possible. Seal tightly and store in the refrigerator to marinate overnight.

4. Preheat a large grill pan over medium-high heat.

5. Remove the meat from the marinade and place it on a plate. Season both sides with the salt and pepper.

6. Working in batches so the meat browns nicely, place 4 or 5 pieces of meat flat on the grill, making sure they're not overlapping. Cook the first side for 3 minutes. Flip and cook the second side for another 4 minutes. (This will give you medium done meat.) Remove and set aside on a plate. Repeat until all the meat is cooked.

7. Divide the meat into two portions—one for the refrigerator and the other for the freezer.

jenny's tip

I recommend cooking the Carne Asada to medium doneness so it's nice and tender. The meat should still be okay texture-wise if you cook it a little bit longer because both chuck and skirt steak are generally fatty cuts of meat.

Approximate macros per serving:
Calories: **350** • Fat: **26g** • Protein: **22g** • Net Carbs: **6g** • Fiber: **1g**

Chicken Adobo

SERVES 8 · **PREP TIME:** 15 minutes · **COOK TIME:** 35 minutes

Chicken Adobo was the first Filipino dish I made for Will (and the first he'd ever tried!), so I was stoked when he gave it two thumbs up and ate two servings for dinner. This classic Filipino dish has simple ingredients that you can turn into a flavorful and delicious meal in less than an hour. The chicken tastes better the longer it sits in the refrigerator (thanks to the vinegar), and you won't get tired of eating it again and again. Pan-frying the cooked chicken for a few minutes caramelizes the skin to make the dish taste out of this world!

1 whole chicken (about 4½ pounds), cut into pieces

¾ cup apple cider vinegar

¾ cup coconut aminos

1 (1-inch) piece ginger, peeled and sliced

8 cloves garlic, minced (about 8 teaspoons)

2 teaspoons sea salt

2 teaspoons black pepper

5 bay leaves

½ cup full-fat coconut milk

4 bird's eye chili peppers (optional)

1. Put the chicken pieces in a large stockpot or Dutch oven. Don't turn on the heat.

2. Pour the apple cider vinegar and coconut aminos over the chicken. Season with the salt and pepper, and arrange the ginger, garlic, and bay leaves evenly on top of the chicken.

3. Turn on the heat to medium-high. Leave the pot uncovered and bring it to a boil.

4. Once it starts to boil, cover the pot and reduce the heat to medium-low. Let the chicken simmer for 20 to 25 minutes, until it's cooked through and the juices run clear when a fork is inserted in the thickest piece of chicken, such as in a breast or thigh.

5. Add the coconut milk and bird's eye chili peppers (if using). Stir to combine. Simmer, uncovered, until the sauce is reduced by half, 8 to 10 minutes, stirring halfway through.

6. Divide the chicken and sauce into two portions. One will be refrigerated and the other will be frozen.

Substitute 4 pounds of drumsticks if you prefer not to cut up a whole chicken. This will reduce the prep time by 10 minutes.

Transfer one portion of the chicken with sauce to a glass container, cover, and store in the refrigerator for up to 1 week.

Discard the bird's eye chili peppers and bay leaves before transferring the second portion of chicken and sauce to a zip-top freezer bag. Gently squeeze the bag to remove any excess air before sealing. Store in the freezer for up to 3 months.

Move the bag of frozen chicken to the refrigerator and let it thaw overnight. Reheat the chicken and sauce in the microwave on high for 3 to 4 minutes.

Approximate macros per serving:
Calories: **225** · Fat: **11g** · Protein: **13g** · Net Carbs: **10g** · Fiber: **1g**

Blanched Bok Choy

SERVES 4 • **PREP TIME:** 1 minute • **COOK TIME:** 3 minutes

Bok choy is a mild vegetable that is usually added to stir-fries. Blanching it for a few minutes quickly cooks it while maintaining its bright green color.

1 teaspoon sea salt

1 pound baby bok choy, cut in half lengthwise

1. Fill a medium-sized stockpot halfway with water and bring to a boil over high heat.

2. Add the salt and stir with a spoon for a few seconds until the salt dissolves.

3. Add the bok choy and blanch for 3 minutes.

4. Immediately remove the bok choy from the water and transfer it to a colander to drain completely.

Line a glass container with 2 sheets of paper towel. Place the bok choy on top of the paper towels, cover the container, and store in the refrigerator for up to 5 days. The paper towels will help absorb excess moisture from the bok choy.

Approximate macros per serving: ———
Calories: **16** • Fat: **1g** • Protein: **1g** • Net Carbs: **1g** • Fiber: **1g**

Zesty Slaw

SERVES 4 • **PREP TIME:** 15 minutes, plus 30 minutes to refrigerate
COOK TIME: —

Since going keto, I've found that eating a serving of slaw helps keep me full while adding a good amount of vegetables to my meal. Slaw also satisfies my craving for something crunchy! This Zesty Slaw has a little bit of a kick and goes great with any type of grilled meat.

Don't have time to shred whole heads of cabbage? Use bagged shredded coleslaw instead and save about 10 minutes of prep time.

Transfer the slaw to a glass container, cover, and store in the refrigerator for up to 5 days.

Jenny's tip

Six cups of shredded cabbage sounds like a lot, but the acidity of the dressing softens it, so your finished slaw reduces to about 4 cups after you've refrigerated it.

FOR THE DRESSING:

1 cup stemmed and finely chopped fresh cilantro

3 cloves garlic, minced (about 3 teaspoons)

Juice of 2 limes (about ¼ cup)

3 jalapeño peppers, seeded and finely chopped

1 teaspoon sea salt

¼ cup plus 2 tablespoons olive oil

½ head green cabbage, shredded (about 3 cups)

½ head red cabbage, shredded (about 3 cups)

1. Put the ingredients for the dressing in a small bowl and stir to combine.

2. Put the shredded green cabbage and red cabbage in a large bowl. Pour the dressing over the cabbage and use two forks to toss until it's well coated. Cover the bowl with plastic wrap and refrigerate for 30 minutes to allow the flavors to blend.

Approximate macros per serving:
Calories: **271** • Fat: **21g** • Protein: **2g** • Net Carbs: **10g** • Fiber: **6g**

Balsamic Roasted Tomatoes

 Transfer the cooled tomatoes to a glass container, cover, and store in the refrigerator for up to 5 days.

SERVES 4 • **PREP TIME:** 5 minutes • **COOK TIME:** 27 minutes

Roasting tomatoes in the oven brings out their natural sweetness, and finishing them by charring the skin under the broiler adds a smokiness that complements the sweet and sour elements of the balsamic vinegar.

3 (10-ounce) packages cherry tomatoes, halved

1 tablespoon olive oil

2 tablespoons balsamic vinegar

½ teaspoon garlic powder

½ teaspoon onion powder

½ teaspoon sea salt

½ teaspoon black pepper

1. Preheat the oven to 375°F.

2. Place the cherry tomatoes on a rimmed baking sheet. Drizzle the tomatoes with the olive oil and balsamic vinegar, then season with the garlic powder, onion powder, salt, and pepper.

3. Mix well to make sure the oil, vinegar, and seasonings are distributed evenly.

4. Bake the tomatoes until the skins are soft and shriveled, about 25 minutes.

5. Turn the oven to broil and broil the tomatoes for 2 minutes to give them a nice caramelized crust.

Approximate macros per serving:
Calories: **93** • Fat: **4g** • Protein: **2g** • Net Carbs: **7g** • Fiber: **3g**

Turmeric Garlic Cauliflower Rice

SERVES 4 • **PREP TIME:** 10 minutes • **COOK TIME:** 10 minutes

Transfer the rice to a glass container, cover, and store in the refrigerator for up to 5 days.

Adding turmeric to cauliflower rice gives it a nice, bright color that's visually appealing and makes it fun to eat. Turmeric helps a lot with inflammation, and combining it with garlic boosts the nutrients of this cauliflower rice. You can thaw the frozen riced cauliflower quickly by placing the bags on a paper towel–lined chopping board at room temperature. Using high heat and a dry pan helps the excess water evaporate quickly and keeps the rice from turning mushy. You also end up with browned bits of cauliflower that makes the rice taste yummier.

jenny's tip

Skip the thawing step by using fresh riced cauliflower.

2 (12-ounce) bags frozen riced cauliflower

1 tablespoon garlic powder

2 teaspoons turmeric powder

½ teaspoon sea salt

1. Remove the bags of cauliflower from the freezer and set them on a paper towel–lined cutting board. Let thaw for 10 minutes.

2. Heat a cast-iron pan over high heat.

3. Place the cauliflower rice in the pan. Using the back of a wooden spoon, gently break down any large chunks of cauliflower. Let it cook for 2 minutes.

4. Once there are no more frozen chunks, season the cauliflower rice with the garlic powder, turmeric powder, and salt. Stir to mix the seasonings with the cauliflower rice. Let it cook for 6 to 8 minutes, until the rice begins to brown, stirring halfway so it doesn't burn on the bottom.

5. Remove from the pan immediately.

Approximate macros per serving:
Calories: **51** • Fat: **0g** • Protein: **5g** • Net Carbs: **6g** • Fiber: **4g**

Roasted Sweet Peppers and Onions

SERVES 4 • **PREP TIME:** 10 minutes • **COOK TIME:** 35 minutes

Transfer the cooled sweet peppers and onions to a glass container, cover, and store in the refrigerator for up to 5 days.

Roasting sweet peppers and onions together creates an aromatic fajitalike side dish that is pure savory goodness. This side pairs perfectly with the Crispy Carnitas (page 96) or the Carne Asada (page 100).

1 pound mini sweet peppers, halved lengthwise

1 small onion, sliced

1 tablespoon olive oil

½ teaspoon sea salt

½ teaspoon black pepper

1. Preheat the oven to 375°F.
2. Place the peppers and onion slices on a rimmed baking sheet.
3. Drizzle the veggies with the olive oil and season with the salt and pepper.
4. Toss everything together using your hands. Arrange the veggies in a single layer so they cook evenly.
5. Bake for 20 minutes.
6. Remove the pan from the oven and flip over each piece of pepper and onion to allow them to cook evenly on both sides.
7. Bake for another 15 minutes, until the peppers are soft and slightly browned.

Approximate macros per serving: ⎯⎯⎯⎯⎯⎯⎯⎯⎯
Calories: **82** • Fat: **4g** • Protein: **2g** • Net Carbs: **7g** • Fiber: **3g**

Zucchini Noodles

SERVES 8 • **PREP TIME:** 5 minutes, plus 20 minutes to let the noodles drain • **COOK TIME:** 1 minute

Salting raw zucchini noodles helps draw out excess liquid and prevents them from being soggy and watered down after cooking. Four pounds looks like a lot of zucchini, but the noodles will shrink considerably, so a serving ends up being about ¾ cup.

8 large zucchini (about 4 pounds), spiral-sliced into noodles

1 teaspoon sea salt

Olive oil spray

1. Place the zucchini noodles on a rimmed baking sheet. Season with the salt and mix well using your hands. Arrange the noodles evenly on the baking sheet. Let the noodles sit for 20 minutes to allow the excess water to drain.

2. Transfer the noodles to a paper towel–lined cutting board. Gently pat the noodles dry with additional paper towels.

3. Heat a large cast-iron pan over high heat. Coat the pan lightly with the olive oil spray. Add the zucchini noodles and sauté for 1 minute.

If you don't own a spiralizer or want to save about 5 minutes of prep time, you can find ready-to-use spiral-sliced zucchini noodles at most grocery stores.

Line a glass container with two sheets of paper towel, which will absorb excess liquid produced by the zucchini. Place the zucchini noodles on top, cover, and store in the refrigerator for up to 5 days.

Approximate macros per serving: Calories: **40** • Fat: **0g** • Protein: **1g** • Net Carbs: **6g** • Fiber: **3g**

Chili Oil

YIELD: ½ cup, 1 tablespoon per serving • **PREP TIME:** 2 minutes
COOK TIME: 1 minute

Chili oil is a popular condiment in Asian cuisine and adds a good amount of heat to soups, eggs, grilled meat, and just about anything else. You can control the spice level by adjusting the quantity of chili flakes you use. I always have a jar of chili oil in my pantry, so it's ready to use any time I need it!

½ cup olive oil

1 tablespoon red pepper flakes

⅛ teaspoon paprika

1 tablespoon toasted sesame oil

1. Place a small saucepan over medium heat.

2. Pour in the olive oil and heat for 1 minute. The oil should be hot but not smoking.

3. Turn off the heat and add the red pepper flakes and paprika. Let the mixture steep for 3 minutes.

4. Add the sesame oil and mix well. Let cool for 5 minutes.

Transfer the chili oil to a jar. Let cool completely before covering it with the lid. Store in the pantry for up to 3 months.

jenny's tip

Double the amount of red pepper flakes for a spicier chili oil!

Approximate macros per serving: ─────────
Calories: **137** • Fat: **15g** • Protein: **0g** • Net Carbs: **0g** • Fiber: **0g**

Pico de Gallo

YIELD: 2 cups, ¼ cup per serving • **PREP TIME:** 15 minutes
COOK TIME: —

A batch of this pico de gallo tastes great on eggs, avocados, vegetables, and meat. It will produce a little bit of liquid as it sits in the refrigerator, but it still tastes great by the end of the week.

4 Roma tomatoes, chopped

½ small onion, chopped

1 jalapeño pepper, seeded and chopped

¼ cup chopped fresh cilantro

Juice of 1 lime (about 2 tablespoons)

½ teaspoon sea salt

Place all the ingredients in a large bowl and stir to mix everything together. Taste and add more salt, if desired.

Buy premade salsa with clean ingredients to skip preparing homemade pico de gallo and save about 15 minutes of prep time.

Transfer to a jar and cover tightly. Store in the refrigerator for up to 5 days.

Approximate macros per serving: ——————————
Calories: **27** • Fat: **0g** • Protein: **1g** • Net Carbs: **2g** • Fiber: **2g**

Build Your Plate

Loaded Hamburger Hash
with sliced avocado

1. Heat two servings of the Loaded Hamburger Hash (page 90) in the microwave on high for 1 to 2 minutes or in a skillet over medium heat for 3 minutes.

2. Divide the hash between two plates.

3. Slice one avocado, then top each serving of hash with half of the avocado slices. Sprinkle a little shaved Parmesan cheese on top of each serving.

Savory Breakfast Plate

1. Heat two servings of the Balsamic Roasted Tomatoes (page 108) and two beef hot dogs in the microwave on high for 1 minute.

2. Divide the tomatoes and hot dogs between two plates.

3. Slice one avocado and place half on each plate. Add a cup of baby arugula to each plate.

Turkey Mushroom Sauté,
Blanched Bok Choy, Chili Oil

1. Heat two servings of the Turkey Mushroom Sauté (page 94) and Blanched Bok Choy (page 104) in the microwave on high for 1 to 2 minutes or in a skillet over medium heat for 2 minutes.

2. Divide the turkey sauté and bok choy between two plates.

3. Drizzle 1 tablespoon of the Chili Oil (page 116) on top of each serving of the Turkey Mushroom Sauté.

Crispy Carnitas, Zesty Slaw, Pico de Gallo

1. Heat two servings of the Crispy Carnitas (page 96) in a skillet over medium-high heat for 3 minutes or until the pork pieces are crispy.

2. Divide the pork between two plates. Add one serving of the Zesty Slaw (page 106) and ¼ cup of Pico de Gallo (page 118) to each plate.

Carne Asada, Roasted Sweet Peppers and Onion, Pico de Gallo, Limes

1. Heat two servings of the Carne Asada (page 100) and Roasted Sweet Peppers and Onions (page 112) in a skillet over medium-high heat for 3 to 4 minutes.
2. Divide the meat and vegetables between two plates.
3. Add ¼ cup of the Pico de Gallo (page 118) to the plate and serve with half a lime on the side.

Pesto Meatballs, Zucchini Noodles, Parmesan Cheese

1. Heat two servings of the Zucchini Noodles (page 114) in a skillet over medium heat for 1 minute.
2. Divide the noodles between two plates.
3. Heat two servings of the Pesto Meatballs (page 98) in a skillet over medium heat for 2 minutes.
4. Place the meatballs on top of the noodles and sprinkle Parmesan cheese on top.

Chicken Adobo, Turmeric Garlic Cauliflower Rice

Plate two servings of the Turmeric Garlic Cauliflower Rice (page 110). Top each serving with the Chicken Adobo (page 102) and a tablespoon of the sauce. Microwave on high for 3 to 4 minutes.

WEEK 3

Getting Started

Two weeks down, two more to go! Not only are you mastering the art of meal prepping but you're also beginning to stock your freezer with ready-to-eat meals that you can enjoy later, either as a last-minute meal or as part of a meal plan. You'll be using your Instant Pot this week, so if you haven't had a chance to use it, the Instant Pot Roast (page 146) is an easy recipe to start with!

Print the downloadable week 3 PDF from **easyketomealprep.com/week3.**

What's on the Menu

If you need to adjust the quantities of the recipes for your needs, see the table on page 33 in the "What's on the Menu" section in the Introduction for more information.

MAIN DISHES

Shortcut Shakshuka

COOKING METHOD:
PREP TIME: 5 minutes
COOK TIME: 19 minutes
SERVES 6

Sheet Pan Cauliflower Fried Rice

COOKING METHOD:
PREP TIME: 5 minutes
COOK TIME: 25 minutes
SERVES 4

Filipino Turbo Chicken

COOKING METHOD:
PREP TIME: 10 minutes
COOK TIME: 45 minutes
SERVES 4

Wonton Noodle Soup

COOKING METHOD:
PREP TIME: 10 minutes
COOK TIME: 20 minutes
SERVES 4

Cheeseburger Casserole

COOKING METHOD:
PREP TIME: 5 minutes
COOK TIME: 40 minutes
SERVES 4

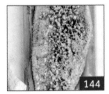

Baked Salmon

COOKING METHOD:
PREP TIME: 2 minutes
COOK TIME: 20 minutes
SERVES 4

Instant Pot Roast

COOKING METHOD:
PREP TIME: 2 minutes
COOK TIME: 75 minutes
SERVES 8

save half for later

The Instant Pot Roast (page 146) makes enough so that you easily can freeze extras and use them later for Pork Rind Nachos (page 270) as a super-filling snack! The Filipino Turbo Chicken (page 138) and Wonton Noodle Soup (page 140) are freezer-friendly as well.

jenny's meal prep tip

Keep Your Fridge Clean

Each week, check your refrigerator for any leftover food that has been in there for more than a week and throw it out. Keeping your refrigerator clean and clutter-free means that you'll have space to store your new batch of ready-to-eat meals.

Also, don't forget to check the expiration dates of refrigerated condiments once every couple of months to make sure they're still safe to eat!

SIDES

Mediterranean Couscous

COOKING METHOD:
PREP TIME: 10 minutes
COOK TIME: 2 minutes
SERVES 6

Nutty Tahini Broccoli

COOKING METHOD:
PREP TIME: 5 minutes
COOK TIME: 30 minutes
SERVES 4

Three-Veggie Chop Suey

COOKING METHOD:
PREP TIME: 10 minutes
COOK TIME: 6 minutes
SERVES 4

Shredded Kale and Pepita Pecan Salad

COOKING METHOD: —
PREP TIME: 15 minutes
COOK TIME: —
SERVES 4

Jalapeño Cauliflower Mash

COOKING METHOD:
PREP TIME: 2 minutes
COOK TIME: 15 minutes
SERVES 4

CONDIMENTS AND GARNISHES

Pan-Roasted Garlic Oil

COOKING METHOD:
PREP TIME: 1 minute
COOK TIME: 6 minutes
YIELD: 1 cup

Olive Gremolata

COOKING METHOD: —
PREP TIME: 15 minutes
COOK TIME: —
YIELD: 1 cup

Steak Rub

COOKING METHOD: —
PREP TIME: 2 minutes
COOK TIME: —
YIELD: 3 tablespoons

Meal Plan

Cook Once a Week

DAY	BREAKFAST	LUNCH	DINNER
1	Shortcut Shakshuka, Mediterranean Couscous, Pan-Roasted Garlic Oil	Baked Salmon, Olive Gremolata, Nutty Tahini Broccoli	Filipino Turbo Chicken, Three-Veggie Chop Suey
2	Sheet Pan Cauliflower Fried Rice	Cheeseburger Casserole, Shredded Kale and Pepita Pecan Salad	Baked Salmon, Olive Gremolata, Nutty Tahini Broccoli
3	Shortcut Shakshuka, Mediterranean Couscous, Pan-Roasted Garlic Oil	Filipino Turbo Chicken, Three-Veggie Chop Suey	Cheeseburger Casserole, Shredded Kale and Pepita Pecan Salad
4	Sheet Pan Cauliflower Fried Rice	Wonton Noodle Soup	Instant Pot Roast, Steak Rub, Jalapeño Cauliflower Mash, Pan-Roasted Garlic Oil
5	Shortcut Shakshuka, Mediterranean Couscous, Pan-Roasted Garlic Oil	Instant Pot Roast, Steak Rub, Jalapeño Cauliflower Mash, Pan-Roasted Garlic Oil	Wonton Noodle Soup
6	Free Meal	Leftovers	Leftovers
7	Free Meal	Leftovers	Leftovers

Cook Twice a Week

DAY	BREAKFAST	LUNCH	DINNER
1	Shortcut Shakshuka, Mediterranean Couscous, Pan-Roasted Garlic Oil	Filipino Turbo Chicken, Three-Veggie Chop Suey	Wonton Noodle Soup
2	Shortcut Shakshuka, Mediterranean Couscous, Pan-Roasted Garlic Oil	Wonton Noodle Soup	Instant Pot Roast, Steak Rub, Jalapeño Cauliflower Mash, Pan-Roasted Garlic Oil
3	Shortcut Shakshuka, Mediterranean Couscous, Pan-Roasted Garlic Oil	Filipino Turbo Chicken, Three-Veggie Chop Suey	Baked Salmon, Olive Gremolata, Nutty Tahini Broccoli
4	Sheet Pan Cauliflower Fried Rice	Cheeseburger Casserole, Shredded Kale and Pepita Pecan Salad	Instant Pot Roast, Steak Rub, Jalapeño Cauliflower Mash, Pan-Roasted Garlic Oil
5	Sheet Pan Cauliflower Fried Rice	Baked Salmon, Olive Gremolata, Nutty Tahini Broccoli	Cheeseburger Casserole, Shredded Kale and Pepita Pecan Salad
6	Free Meal	Leftovers	Leftovers
7	Free Meal	Leftovers	Leftovers

Grocery List

In Your Pantry

Avocado oil, ¼ cup plus 1 tablespoon

Black pepper, 1½ teaspoons

Coconut milk, full-fat, 1 cup

Coconut aminos, ¾ cup

Fish sauce, 1½ tablespoons

Garlic powder, 1½ teaspoons

Ghee, ¼ cup plus 2 teaspoons

Ground cumin, ½ teaspoon

Olive oil, 1½ cups

Olive oil spray

Onion powder, ½ teaspoon

Paprika, 2 teaspoons

Sea salt, 1½ tablespoons

Toasted sesame oil, 2 tablespoons

*Do you need to replenish any pantry items this week? Add them to your grocery list. You can print the downloadable list from **easyketomealprep.com/pantry** to take with you to the grocery store. Check off all the items under the In Your Pantry category because these are already on the Pantry Essentials list.*

Other Items

Broth, beef, 1 (16-ounce) carton

Broth, chicken, 1 (16-ounce) carton

Marinara sauce, 1 (12-ounce) jar and 1 (26-ounce) jar

Olives, Castelvetrano, pitted, 1 cup

Pecan halves, raw, ½ cup

Pepitas, raw, ¼ cup

Shirataki noodles, 2 (8-ounce) packages

You can substitute any type of spaghetti sauce, such as roasted garlic or basil, for the marinara.

You can use Cerignola olives if the Castelvetrano variety isn't available. Both are mild green olives to use in the gremolata.

Condiments and Spices

Black pepper, cracked, 2 teaspoons

Cayenne pepper, ¼ teaspoon

Coarse sea salt, 2 teaspoons

Dried rosemary, ½ teaspoon

Sesame seeds, 1 tablespoon

Tahini, ½ cup

White pepper, ground, 1½ teaspoons

Worcestershire sauce, 1 tablespoon plus 1 teaspoon

Swap 1 jar of ready-made steak rub for the coarse sea salt, cracked black pepper, paprika, onion powder, garlic powder, and dried rosemary.

Eggs and Dairy

Eggs, large, 9

Feta cheese, crumbled, ½ cup

Goat's milk cheddar cheese, 8 ounces

Grab some fresh goat cheese or sheep's milk cheese if you can't find goat's milk cheddar.

Produce

Baby bok choy, 6 ounces

Bell pepper (any color), 1

Broccoli florets, 1 pound

Cabbage, napa, 1 pound

Carrots, shredded, 1 (10-ounce) bag

Cauliflower, riced fresh, 2 pounds

Cauliflower florets, 1 pound

Cilantro, 1 bunch

Garlic, 19 cloves (about 2 bulbs)

Green onions, 1 bunch

Jalapeño pepper, 1

Kale, lacinato, 1 bunch

Lemons, 6

Lemongrass, 3 ounces (3 stalks)

Limes, 2

Parsley, curly or Italian, 2 bunches

Radishes, 1 bunch

Shallot, 1

Snow peas, 6 ounces

Swap 1 (8-ounce) bag of shredded kale for the 1 bunch of lacinato kale.

Meat and Seafood

Andouille sausage links, 4 (1 pound)

Beef, boneless chuck roast, 2½ pounds

Beef, ground, 1 pound

Chicken drumsticks, 3 pounds

Pork, ground, 1 pound

Shrimp, raw, 4 ounces

Wild salmon fillet, 1 pound

Meal Prep Game Plan

ESTIMATED TIME SPENT: 15 minutes

1. Read and review the week's menu, grocery list, meal plan, and recipes. Print the downloadable PDF for the week.

   If you want to include keto-friendly snacks or treats to your meal plan for the week, add the ingredients you need to the Other Items category of your grocery list. Some ideas for this week are Pepperoni Pizza Bites (page 252), Nutty Chia Pudding (page 274), and Chocolate Bark (page 276).

2. Review the In Your Pantry section of the grocery list and check off any items that you already have on hand. Be sure you have enough of each pantry item for the recipes you will prepare on meal prep day.

3. Review the Prep Time-Savers, Substitutions, and Dairy Options sections of the grocery list.

   You can buy the convenience items suggested to help cut your prep time this week. Cross off the ingredients that each convenience item replaces on the grocery list.

   Mark ingredients that you need to substitute for; also take note of your preferred dairy option and indicate your choice.

4. Check your calendar for family/work/social events in the coming week. Mark any meals when you won't be eating your prepared dishes. Swap these meals with Leftovers or a Free Meal.

ESTIMATED TIME SPENT: 45 minutes

Shop for groceries. Don't forget your printed grocery list (and Pantry Essentials list if you're shopping for both).

ESTIMATED TIME SPENT: 1 hour

POWER HOUR PREP

1. Prepare the following components if you decide not to buy a premade steak rub:
   - Pan-Roasted Garlic Oil (page 158)
   - Olive Gremolata (page 160)
   - Steak Rub (page 162)

2. Prep and marinate the Filipino Turbo Chicken (page 138).

3. Prep the aromatics and vegetables. Store each aromatic separately in a zip-top plastic bag or airtight glass container in the refrigerator:
   - Mince 13 cloves of garlic (about ¼ cup and 1 teaspoon).
   - Slice 3 stalks of lemongrass.
   - Chop 1 bunch of kale into thin strips.
   - Chop 1 bunch of parsley.
   - Slice 1 head of napa cabbage.
   - Slice 1 bunch of radishes.

Cook Once a Week

You should be feeling more confident with meal prepping this week and starting to refine your technique in the kitchen. There are equal numbers of stove and oven recipes, plus one for the Instant Pot. The majority of the oven recipes use the same temperature, so you can cook multiple dishes at the same time!

Cool each cooked dish for 10 to 15 minutes before transferring to the containers specified in the 🅷 *Refrigerate This section of the recipes.*

MEAL PREP DAY

1	Arrange two racks toward the middle of the oven and preheat the oven to 375°F. Bake the Sheet Pan Cauliflower Fried Rice (page 136) on the bottom rack and the Filipino Turbo Chicken (page 138) on the top rack.
2	While the fried rice and chicken are in the oven, cook the Instant Pot Roast (page 146) in the pressure cooker. Cook the Mediterranean Couscous (page 148) on the stove. The Sheet Pan Cauliflower Fried Rice should be ready to finish at this point. Temporarily remove the chicken from the oven and move the fried rice to the top rack. Turn the oven to a high temperature and broil for 5 minutes. Remove the fried rice from the oven. Reset the oven to 375°F and place the chicken back on the top rack to continue cooking.
3	Bake the Baked Salmon (page 144) on the bottom rack of the oven.
4	Cook the Jalapeño Cauliflower Mash (page 156) on the stove. When the mash is done, the chicken and salmon should be done baking. Remove the salmon from the oven, turn the oven to a high temperature, and broil the chicken on high for 5 minutes. Remove the chicken from the oven and reset the temperature to 375°F.
5	Cook the ground beef for Cheeseburger Casserole (page 142) on the stove, add the sauce, and let it simmer. After adding the other ingredients, transfer the casserole to the top rack in the oven to bake. Simmer the sauce for the Shortcut Shakshuka (page 134) on the stove, then add the eggs and transfer the pan to the bottom rack of the oven to finish cooking.
6	Cook the Wonton Noodle Soup (page 140) on the stove. While the soup is simmering, cook the Three-Veggie Chop Suey (page 152) on the stove. The Shortcut Shakshuka should be done at this point. Remove it from the oven.
7	Prepare the Shredded Kale and Pepita Pecan Salad (page 154).
8	Remove the Cheeseburger Casserole from the oven and increase the temperature to 400°F. Roast the Nutty Tahini Broccoli (page 150) in the oven.

Cook Twice a Week

MEAL PREP DAY 1: START OF THE WEEK

1	Arrange two racks in the middle of the oven and preheat the oven to 375°F.
	Bake the Filipino Turbo Chicken (page 138) on the top rack.
	Simmer the sauce for the Shortcut Shakshuka (page 134) on the stove, then add the eggs and transfer the pan to the bottom rack of the oven to finish cooking.
2	While the chicken and shakshuka are in the oven, cook the Instant Pot Roast (page 146) in the pressure cooker.
3	Cook the Wonton Noodle Soup (page 140) on the stove.
	While the soup is simmering, cook the Three-Veggie Chop Suey (page 152) on the stove.
	The Shortcut Shakshuka should be done at this point. Remove it from the oven.
4	Cook the Jalapeño Cauliflower Mash (page 156) on the stove.
	When the mash is done, the chicken should be ready to finish. Turn the oven to a high temperature and broil the chicken for 5 minutes. Remove the chicken from the oven and set the oven temperature to 400°F.

MEAL PREP DAY 2: MIDWEEK

1	Arrange two racks in the middle of the oven and preheat the oven to 375°F.
	Bake the Sheet Pan Cauliflower Fried Rice (page 136) on the top rack of the oven.
2	Bake the Baked Salmon (page 144) on the bottom rack of the oven at the same time as the fried rice.
3	Prepare the Shredded Kale and Pepita Pecan Salad (page 154).
	The fried rice and salmon should be done at this point. Remove the salmon from the oven, turn the temperature to high, and broil the fried rice for 5 minutes. Remove the fried rice from the oven and reset the temperature to 375°F.
4	Cook the ground beef for the Cheeseburger Casserole (page 142) on the stove, add the sauce, and let it simmer. After adding the other ingredients, transfer the casserole to the top rack of the oven to bake.
5	Once the casserole is done, increase the oven temperature to 400°F.
	Roast the Nutty Tahini Broccoli (page 150) in the oven.

My Week 3 Meal Prep Notes

Shortcut Shakshuka

SERVES 6 · **PREP TIME:** 5 minutes · **COOK TIME:** 19 minutes

 Transfer the shakshuka to a glass container. Cover and store in the refrigerator for up to 5 days.

jenny's tip

If you prefer firmer yolks, add 2 minutes to the oven cooking time.

When I first tried shakshuka, I expected it to be this super complicated, fancy dish because of its name. Turns out that it's a just a combination of eggs, tomatoes, and spices! I created a shortcut version using ready-made marinara sauce to shorten the simmering time while achieving a rich, hearty flavor.

2 teaspoons ghee

3 cloves garlic, minced (about 3 teaspoons)

1 (26-ounce) jar marinara sauce

1 teaspoon paprika

½ teaspoon ground cumin

¼ teaspoon cayenne pepper

6 large eggs

FOR THE TOPPINGS:

¼ cup crumbled feta cheese

½ teaspoon black pepper

¼ cup chopped fresh Italian or curly parsley

2 tablespoons Pan-Roasted Garlic Oil (page 158), for serving

1. Preheat the oven to 375°F.
2. Melt the ghee in a large cast-iron pan over medium-high heat.
3. Add the garlic and sauté for 1 minute, until lightly browned.
4. Pour in the marinara sauce and season with the paprika, cumin, and cayenne pepper. Stir to distribute the seasonings and reduce the heat to medium. Let simmer for 8 minutes.
5. Create 6 wells in the sauce and gently crack an egg into each well.
6. Transfer the pan to the oven and bake for 8 to 10 minutes, until the egg whites are set but the yolks are still soft.
7. Top with the feta cheese, pepper, parsley, and Pan-Roasted Garlic Oil.

Approximate macros per serving:
Calories: **190** · Fat: **14g** · Protein: **9g** · Net Carbs: **6g** · Fiber: **1g**

Sheet Pan Cauliflower Fried Rice

SERVES 4 • **PREP TIME:** 5 minutes • **COOK TIME:** 25 minutes

Transfer the Cauliflower Fried Rice to a glass container, cover, and store in the refrigerator for up to 5 days.

Jenny's tip

Chicken sausage is a great alternative for this recipe, and any flavor will work. Andouille is my go-to, but feel free to use your favorite!

I usually stir-fry cauliflower rice on the stove, but I wanted a hands-off method so I could let the oven do all the work! The combination of ingredients in this recipe was inspired by a trip to Hawaii that I took with my mom and brother. While we were there, we ate fried rice and sausages for breakfast. Tossing in cilantro at the very end gives the dish that mmmm factor!

Olive oil spray

1 pound fresh riced cauliflower

4 links (1 pound) andouille sausage, cooked and sliced into rounds

2 large eggs, whisked

2 green onions, chopped

2 tablespoons coconut aminos

1 teaspoon garlic powder

¼ cup chopped fresh cilantro

1. Preheat the oven to 375°F. Lightly coat a rimmed baking sheet with the olive oil spray.

2. Combine the riced cauliflower, sausage, eggs, green onions, coconut aminos, and garlic powder. Mix well to distribute the egg and seasonings evenly.

3. Transfer the cauliflower and sausage mixture to the middle of the prepared baking sheet and use a spatula to spread it evenly.

4. Bake for 15 to 20 minutes, until the rice has softened and the eggs are set and firm.

5. Remove the pan from the oven, give the rice and sausage mixture a quick stir, and turn the oven to broil. Return the pan to the oven and broil for 5 minutes to give the rice a nice browned crust. Sprinkle the cilantro on top and stir.

Approximate macros per serving: ─────────
Calories: **129** • Fat: **8g** • Protein: **9g** • Net Carbs: **4g** • Fiber: **3g**

Filipino Turbo Chicken

SERVES 4 • **PREP TIME:** 10 minutes, plus time to marinate overnight
COOK TIME: 45 minutes

When I was growing up in the Philippines, my mom made roasted chicken in a portable convection oven called a turbo broiler. It had a clear glass base, which made it fun to watch the chicken cook until the skin turned golden brown. The marinade for this recipe is a combination of lemon juice, lime juice, and coconut aminos, which is pretty close to the calamansi and soy sauce mixture my mom used. The lemongrass gives it a nice aroma and fun twist!

FOR THE MARINADE:

1 shallot, sliced

3 ounces lemongrass, sliced (about 3 stalks)

6 cloves garlic, minced (about 6 teaspoons)

½ cup coconut aminos

Juice of 2 lemons (about ¼ cup)

Juice of 2 limes (about ¼ cup)

1 tablespoon fish sauce

3 pounds chicken drumsticks

Olive oil spray

1. Combine the marinade ingredients in a small bowl and mix well.

2. Place the chicken in a large zip-top bag and pour in the marinade.

3. Gently press the bag to remove any excess air before sealing the bag. Place it on the countertop, flip it back and forth, and gently massage it to make sure the marinade coats the chicken. Marinate in the refrigerator overnight.

4. Preheat the oven to 375°F.

5. Line a rimmed baking sheet with foil and lightly coat the foil with the olive oil spray.

6. Remove the chicken from the marinade and arrange it evenly on the prepared baking sheet. Remove the shallot and lemongrass from the marinade and place them on top of the chicken. Discard the excess marinade. Bake for 40 minutes.

7. Turn the oven to broil and broil the chicken for 5 minutes, until the chicken skin turns golden brown.

Transfer the chicken to a glass container. Cover and store in the refrigerator for up to 5 days.

Transfer the chicken to a zip-top freezer bag and gently press the bag to remove any excess air before sealing it. Arrange the chicken in one layer to save space and to allow it to thaw evenly. Store in the freezer for up to 2 months.

Move the bag of frozen chicken to the refrigerator to let it thaw overnight. Reheat in the oven at 375°F for 5 to 8 minutes or in a skillet over medium heat for 5 minutes.

Jenny's tip

For the authentic Filipino experience, use a 3-pound whole chicken and stuff it with the shallot, lemongrass, and garlic before marinating it with the rest of the ingredients. Bake the chicken for 60 to 65 minutes, until the internal temperature at the thickest part is 160°F.

Approximate macros per serving: ——————
Calories: **667** • Fat: **34g** • Protein: **76g** • Net Carbs: **12g** • Fiber: **0g**

Wonton Noodle Soup

SERVES 4 • **PREP TIME:** 10 minutes • **COOK TIME:** 20 minutes

This keto version of one of my childhood comfort foods hits the spot, especially when I am craving a piping hot bowl of noodle soup. When I was experimenting with this recipe, I ate it for dinner for four straight days. No kidding! The broth is rich and hearty, and the noodles are comforting without feeling heavy in your stomach. If you've never tried shirataki noodles, you'll be hooked once you make this recipe; they're the perfect replacement for regular noodles without the calories and carbs!

2 (8-ounce) packages shirataki noodles

1 pound ground pork

4 ounces raw shrimp, peeled and chopped

½ cup chopped green onions

2½ teaspoons ground white pepper, divided

2 teaspoons sea salt, divided

2 cups chicken broth

3 cups water

6 ounces baby bok choy, quartered

1. Empty the shirataki noodles into a colander and rinse with cold water. Repeat a couple more times until you've rinsed off all the liquid from the package . Drain and set aside.

2. In a large bowl, combine the pork, shrimp, green onions, 2 teaspoons of the white pepper, and 1 teaspoon of the salt. Mix well. Use a tablespoon to scoop the mixture and form it into 1-inch meatballs.

3. Pour the chicken broth and water in a large saucepan over medium-high heat and bring to a boil.

4. Cook the meatballs in two batches to avoid overcrowding in the saucepan. Drop the meatballs one by one into the broth and cook for 5 minutes. You'll see the meatballs float to the top as soon as they're done. Use a slotted spoon to remove the cooked meatballs from the broth and set them aside in a medium-sized bowl. Cook the remaining meatballs.

5. Reduce the heat to medium and bring the broth to a simmer. Add the shirataki noodles to the broth and season with the remaining ½ teaspoon of the white pepper and 1 teaspoon of the salt. Simmer for 8 minutes.

6. Return the meatballs to the saucepan and add the baby bok choy. Stir and cook everything together for 2 minutes.

Divide the meatballs, noodles, and bok choy into four 1-quart wide-mouth mason jars. Divide the broth among the jars, cover, and refrigerate for up to 5 days.

Divide the soup into four 1-quart wide-mouth mason jars, making sure there's at least 1 inch of space at the top to allow the liquid some room to expand as it freezes. Cover tightly and store in the freezer for up to 2 months.

Transfer the jars of soup to the refrigerator to let them thaw overnight. Pour the soup in a medium saucepan over medium-high heat and bring to a simmer.

Approximate macros per serving:
Calories: **331** • Fat: **21g** • Protein: **26g** • Net Carbs: **5g** • Fiber: **1g**

Cheeseburger Casserole

SERVES 4 • **PREP TIME:** 5 minutes • **COOK TIME:** 40 minutes

If you can't find goat's milk cheddar cheese, fresh goat cheese or sheep's milk cheese work as alternatives. If you can tolerate cow's milk, use regular cheddar or mozzarella cheese in place of the goat's milk cheddar, and use regular milk in place of the coconut milk.

Buy shredded cheese to save 3 to 4 minutes of prep time.

Cover the baking dish with foil and store in the refrigerator for up to 5 days.

This casserole is a cross between my Easiest Lasagna (page 188) and Weeknight Bolognese (page 64), and it's equally as easy to make. I was lucky to find goat's milk cheddar cheese at the grocery store, but other types of cheese will do, so pick your favorite or refer to the dairy option on the left for recommendations.

1 tablespoon avocado oil

1 pound ground beef

1 (12-ounce) jar marinara sauce

1 large egg

⅓ cup full-fat coconut milk

8 ounces goat's milk cheddar cheese, shredded

1. Preheat the oven to 375°F.

2. Heat a large cast-iron pan over medium-high heat.

3. Pour in the avocado oil and add the ground beef. Cook, stirring with a wooden spoon to crumble the meat so it cooks evenly, for 8 to 10 minutes, until browned.

4. Drain the excess fat from the pan. This will prevent the casserole from being too runny once it's baked.

5. Stir in the marinara sauce and simmer for 10 minutes. Transfer the mixture to an 8-inch square baking dish.

6. Whisk the egg and coconut milk in a small bowl. Mix in the cheese and pour the mixture on top of the ground beef.

7. Transfer the pan to the oven and bake for 20 minutes, until the sauce is bubbly.

Approximate macros per serving: ——————
Calories: **533** • Fat: **37g** • Protein: **42g** • Net Carbs: **9g** • Fiber: **1g**

Baked Salmon

SERVES 4 • **PREP TIME:** 2 minutes • **COOK TIME:** 20 minutes

Salmon is one of my favorite fish because it cooks fairly quickly and doesn't need a lot of seasoning or garnish to make it delicious. Just the basics—salt, pepper, a squeeze of fresh lemon juice—and a quick sear are all it needs! I bumped the salmon in this recipe up a notch by topping it with the Olive Gremolata, which provides a palate-pleasing finishing touch.

1 (1-pound) wild salmon fillet

2 tablespoons ghee, softened

1 teaspoon sea salt

1 teaspoon black pepper

1 cup Olive Gremolata (page 160)

1. Preheat the oven to 375°F. Line a rimmed baking sheet with parchment paper.

2. Place the salmon skin side down in the middle of the prepared baking sheet and coat the top with the ghee.

3. Season with the salt and pepper.

4. Bake for 15 to 20 minutes, until the fish flakes easily with a fork.

5. Top with half of the Olive Gremolata. Save the other half of the gremolata to serve on the side.

Cut the salmon into 4 servings and transfer to a glass container. Cover and store in the refrigerator for up to 2 days.

Jenny's tip

The two types of salmon I usually get are sockeye and King salmon. Sockeye salmon is bright orange when it's raw or cooked, so it's visually appealing and a wonderful fish to serve at gatherings. It has a firm, steaklike texture, so be careful not to overcook it. King salmon, on the other hand, has a light peach color and a buttery taste and texture that literally melts in your mouth. Either type of salmon works well for this recipe!

Approximate macros per serving: ———
Calories: **287** • Fat: **22g** • Protein: **19g** • Net Carbs: **2g** • Fiber: **1g**

Instant Pot Roast

SERVES 8 • **PREP TIME:** 2 minutes, plus 10 minutes to cool
COOK TIME: 75 minutes, plus 25 minutes to release the pressure

The first time I made pot roast I used a slow cooker, and it took forever to cook! I don't want to have to wait that long, especially on meal prep days. When I finally pulled the trigger one Black Friday and bought an Instant Pot, I knew I had to make my pot roast in it. With a quick sear and less than 2 hours in the Instant Pot, the chuck roast had transformed into fork-tender, mouthwatering morsels of meat!

2½ pounds boneless beef chuck roast

1½ tablespoons Steak Rub (page 162)

2 tablespoons avocado oil

½ cup beef broth

4 teaspoons Worcestershire sauce

1. Pat the chuck roast dry with paper towels to help it sear nicely. Rub both sides of the roast with the Steak Rub, pressing it gently into the meat.

2. Select the Sauté setting on the Instant Pot and set it to High. Pour in the avocado oil to heat it for 30 seconds.

3. Sear the chuck roast for 2 minutes on the first side. Flip and sear the second side for another 2 minutes.

4. Pour the broth and Worcestershire sauce on top of the chuck roast.

5. Press the Cancel button on the Instant Pot and switch to the Manual or Pressure Level setting and set it to high pressure. Place the lid on the pot and turn the vent valve to the sealed position. Set the timer to 75 minutes.

6. Once the chuck roast is done cooking, allow the pressure to release naturally for 25 minutes. After the pressure is released, remove the lid from the Instant Pot and let the roast cool for 10 minutes before shredding the beef with two forks.

Transfer the shredded Instant Pot Roast plus half of the liquid produced during cooking to a glass container. Cover and refrigerate for up to 5 days.

Transfer the shredded Instant Pot Roast and half of the cooking liquid to a zip-top freezer bag. Press gently to remove as much air as possible before sealing and then store the bag flat in the freezer for up to 3 months.

Fill a rectangular baking dish with cold water and submerge the bag of pot roast. Place it in the fridge for an hour, changing the water after 30 minutes. Reheat the pot roast in a skillet over medium-high heat for 5 minutes or in the microwave on high for 2 minutes.

jenny's tips

Instead of using forks, place the pot roast in a stand mixer fitted with a flat beater attachment and turn it on medium-low speed for 10 seconds to shred it.

No Instant Pot? Sear the chuck roast on the stove and then transfer the roast to a slow cooker. Cook on the low setting for 8 to 10 hours.

Approximate macros per serving:
Calories: **153** • Fat: **4g** • Protein: **26g** • Net Carbs: **1g** • Fiber: **0g**

Mediterranean Couscous

SERVES 6 • **PREP TIME:** 10 minutes, plus 10 minutes to cool
COOK TIME: 2 minutes

Transfer the Mediterranean Couscous to a glass container, cover, and store in the refrigerator for up to 5 days. The flavors will infuse the couscous the longer it sits in the refrigerator!

Cooking riced cauliflower for a few minutes until it just begins to soften creates a great base for this Mediterranean Couscous. After you mix in colorful veggies and drizzle it with Pan-Roasted Garlic Oil, you have a light and fluffy side for the Shortcut Shakshuka (page 134).

1 pound fresh riced cauliflower

½ cup chopped bell peppers

¼ cup shredded carrots

¼ cup chopped fresh Italian or curly parsley

¼ cup crumbled feta cheese

2 tablespoons Pan-Roasted Garlic Oil (page 158)

jenny's tip

The cooking time for this dish is short, so buy fresh riced cauliflower instead of frozen to avoid any excess liquid. You can find fresh riced cauliflower in the refrigerated or vegetable section at the grocery store. If you have no access to packaged riced cauliflower, grate a head of cauliflower using a box grater or use a food processor with a shredding disc attachment.

1. Heat a large cast-iron pan over high heat.

2. Place the riced cauliflower and bell peppers in the pan and sauté for 2 minutes. Using a dry pan over high heat helps the riced cauliflower turn out fluffy.

3. Remove the pan from the heat and immediately transfer the vegetables to a bowl. Place in the refrigerator to cool for 10 minutes.

4. Mix in the carrots, parsley, and feta and drizzle with the garlic oil. Toss to combine well.

Approximate macros per serving:
Calories: **89** • Fat: **7g** • Protein: **3g** • Net Carbs: **3g** • Fiber: **3g**

Nutty Tahini Broccoli

SERVES 4 • **PREP TIME:** 5 minutes • **COOK TIME:** 30 minutes

Transfer the broccoli to a glass container. Cover and refrigerate for up to 5 days.

I roast broccoli when I get bored with plain blanched broccoli because roasting takes the flavor to a whole different level by creating a caramelized exterior that brings out the broccoli's sweetness. To kick it up a notch, I toss the straight-from-the-oven roasted broccoli with a nutty tahini sauce for the best bite ever!

Olive oil spray

1 pound broccoli florets

¼ teaspoon sea salt

FOR THE TAHINI SAUCE:

½ cup tahini

¼ cup water

1 clove garlic, minced (about 1 teaspoon)

Grated zest and juice of 1 lemon (about 2 tablespoons each)

¼ teaspoon sea salt

1. Preheat the oven to 400°F. Spray a rimmed baking sheet with the olive oil spray.

2. Arrange the broccoli florets evenly in one layer on the baking sheet. Season with the salt and roast for 15 minutes. Flip each floret and roast for an additional 15 minutes.

3. While the broccoli is roasting, place all the ingredients for the tahini sauce in a small bowl. Use a fork or small whisk to mix well.

4. Once the broccoli is done, pour the tahini sauce over the broccoli and toss to coat each floret.

Approximate macros per serving: ─────────
Calories: **209** • Fat: **16g** • Protein: **9g** • Net Carbs: **7g** • Fiber: **6g**

Three-Veggie Chop Suey

SERVES 4 • **PREP TIME:** 10 minutes • **COOK TIME:** 6 minutes

Transfer the chop suey to a glass container. Cover and store in the refrigerator for up to 3 days.

A quick stir-fried vegetable such as this Three-Veggie Chop Suey is great for pairing with any protein. It takes no more than a few minutes to cook, so you'll have a nutritious side in no time!

1 tablespoon avocado oil

4 cups sliced napa cabbage

1 cup thinly sliced radishes

6 ounces snow peas

2 tablespoons coconut aminos

2 tablespoons toasted sesame oil

1 tablespoon sesame seeds

1 teaspoon fish sauce

¼ teaspoon sea salt

1. Heat a wok or large deep skillet over high heat.

2. Pour in the avocado oil and swirl it over the bottom of the wok. Once it begins to smoke, add the cabbage, radishes, and snow peas. Sauté for 5 minutes.

3. Season with the coconut aminos, sesame oil, sesame seeds, fish sauce, and salt. Toss for 1 minute, then immediately remove from the heat.

Approximate macros per serving: —————
Calories: **148** • Fat: **12g** • Protein: **3g** • Net Carbs: **7g** • Fiber: **2g**

Shredded Kale and Pepita Pecan Salad

SERVES 4 • **PREP TIME:** 15 minutes • **COOK TIME:** —

Transfer the salad to a glass container. Cover and store in the refrigerator for up to 3 days.

Jenny's tip

Refrigerating the salad causes the nuts and seeds to soften a little bit. To preserve their crunch, store the toasted pecans and pepitas in a zip-top bag and sprinkle them on top of the salad when you're ready to eat.

Removing the fibrous stems from the kale and then shredding or chopping the leaves into thin strips creates a palate-pleasing salad base that's perfectly complemented by a light, garlicky lemon dressing and toasted pecans and pepitas. Each bite has the perfect kale-to-nuts ratio, making it a great side dish that even kale haters will enjoy!

½ cup raw pecan halves

¼ cup raw pepitas

3 cups shredded lacinato kale, hard stems removed

¼ cup shredded carrots

Juice of 2 lemons (about ¼ cup)

¼ cup olive oil

1 clove garlic, minced (about 1 teaspoon)

1. Toast the pecans and pepitas in a dry skillet over medium heat for about 8 minutes. Stir every minute to prevent one side from burning. Remove the skillet from the heat and set aside to cool.

2. Place the kale and carrots in a large bowl.

3. In a small bowl, whisk together the lemon juice, olive oil, and garlic. Pour the dressing over the bowl of vegetables and toss well.

4. Mix in the toasted pecans and pepitas.

Approximate macros per serving: —————
Calories: **351** • Fat: **32g** • Protein: **16g** • Net Carbs: **3g** • Fiber: **6g**

Jalapeño Cauliflower Mash

Transfer the cauliflower mash to a glass container. Cover and store in the refrigerator for up to 5 days.

Jenny's tip

If you don't have an immersion blender, transfer the cauliflower and jalapeño to a blender and add the coconut milk and ghee. Cover and puree for 30 seconds. Scrape the sides of the blender and puree for 10 more seconds.

SERVES 4 • **PREP TIME:** 2 minutes • **COOK TIME:** 15 minutes

Cauliflower mash can easily masquerade as regular mashed potatoes because the taste and texture of the two are similar. Throwing in some chopped jalapeño pepper with the cauliflower as it cooks adds a touch of heat and a nice light green hue that makes the dish fun to eat. If you want it muy caliente, you can double the number of jalapeños or even leave the seeds in! Drizzling a little bit of Pan-Roasted Garlic Oil on top enhances the creaminess of this side dish.

1 pound fresh cauliflower florets

1 jalapeño pepper, seeded and chopped

½ cup full-fat coconut milk

2 tablespoons ghee

Sea salt

¼ cup Pan-Roasted Garlic Oil (page 158), for drizzling (optional)

1. Fill a medium-sized saucepan halfway with water and bring to a boil.

2. Place the cauliflower florets and jalapeño pepper in the saucepan and cook for 15 minutes, until you can easily pierce the cauliflower with a fork. Transfer to a colander to drain.

3. Return the cauliflower and jalapeño to the same saucepan and add the coconut milk and ghee. Use an immersion blender to puree everything until it's smooth.

4. Season with salt to taste and mix.

5. Drizzle with the garlic oil, if desired.

Approximate macros per serving:
Calories: **189** • Fat: **16g** • Protein: **3g** • Net Carbs: **8g** • Fiber: **4g**

Pan-Roasted Garlic Oil

YIELD: 1 cup, 1 tablespoon per serving • **PREP TIME:** 1 minute
COOK TIME: 6 minutes

I always have a high-quality olive oil—such as Kasandrinos—in my pantry as one of my main sources of good fat. Infusing the oil with pan-roasted garlic jazzes it up with a toasty, garlicky goodness that'll make you want to pour it over everything!

1 tablespoon avocado oil

6 cloves garlic, smashed, skin on

1 cup olive oil

1. Heat the avocado oil in a small skillet over low heat for 1 minute.

2. Place the garlic cloves in the skillet and stir to coat with the oil. Pan-fry for 3 to 5 minutes on each side, until browned and soft.

3. Turn off the heat and pour the olive oil into the skillet to warm it for 1 minute and infuse the oil with the flavor of the roasted garlic.

4. Carefully remove the skin from the garlic and transfer the peeled garlic cloves to a small jar; pour in the olive oil.

Let the oil cool completely before covering and storing in the pantry at room temperature. The oil will keep for up to 2 weeks.

Approximate macros per serving:
Calories: **129** • Fat: **14g** • Protein: **0g** • Net Carbs: **0g** • Fiber: **0g**

Olive Gremolata

Chop the olives and parsley together in a food processor instead of chopping by hand.

Transfer the Olive Gremolata to a pint-sized wide-mouth mason jar. Cover and store in the refrigerator for up to 5 days.

YIELD: 1 cup, ¼ cup per serving • **PREP TIME:** 15 minutes
COOK TIME: —

Classic gremolata is made from chopped herbs, lemon, and garlic, and you use it as a garnish or finishing touch to meat dishes. I added chopped Castelvetrano olives to this gremolata to give it a nice buttery taste.

1 cup pitted Castelvetrano olives, chopped

Grated zest and juice of 1 lemon (about 2 tablespoons each)

½ cup chopped fresh Italian or curly parsley

2 cloves garlic, minced (about 2 teaspoons)

2 tablespoons olive oil

¼ teaspoon sea salt

Place all the ingredients in a small bowl and mix well.

Jenny's tip

If you can't find Castelvetrano olives, use any other type of mild green olives such as Cerignola.

Approximate macros per serving: ————
Calories: **118** • Fat: **12g** • Protein: **0g** • Net Carbs: **1g** • Fiber: **1g**

Steak Rub

YIELD: 3 tablespoons • **PREP TIME:** 2 minutes • **COOK TIME:** —

Why buy steak rubs with additives and unnecessary ingredients when it's super easy to make your own with just the basics that you have in your spice cabinet? I use this blend on pan-seared rib-eye steaks and chicken tenders. It's also the seasoning for my Instant Pot Roast (page 146). It's good on just about any type of protein!

2 teaspoons coarse sea salt

2 teaspoons cracked black pepper

1 teaspoon paprika

½ teaspoon onion powder

½ teaspoon garlic powder

½ teaspoon dried rosemary, roughly chopped

Combine all the ingredients in a small bowl. Use the steak rub immediately or store it in a tightly covered jar in the pantry for up to 3 months.

Approximate macros per serving: —————
Calories: **6** • Fat: **0g** • Protein: **0g** • Net Carbs: **1g** • Fiber: **0g**

Build Your Plate

Shortcut Shakshuka, Mediterranean Couscous, Pan-Roasted Garlic Oil

1. Heat two servings of the Shortcut Shakshuka (page 134) in the microwave on high for 1 minute.

2. Divide the Shortcut Shakshuka between two plates and add a serving of the Mediterranean Couscous (page 148), which is served cold, to each plate. Drizzle 1 tablespoon of the Pan-Roasted Garlic Oil (page 158) on top of the shakshuka and couscous.

Baked Salmon, Olive Gremolata, Nutty Tahini Broccoli

1. Heat two servings each of the Baked Salmon (page 144) and the Nutty Tahini Broccoli (page 150) in a toaster oven at 350°F for 5 minutes or in a skillet over medium-high heat for 3 minutes.

2. Divide the salmon and broccoli between two plates and top the salmon with a tablespoon of the Olive Gremolata (page 160).

Sheet Pan Cauliflower Fried Rice

1. Heat two servings of the Sheet Pan Cauliflower Fried Rice (page 136) in the microwave on high for 1 minute or in a lightly oiled skillet over medium-high heat for 2 minutes.

2. Divide the cauliflower rice and sausages between two plates.

Filipino Turbo Chicken, Three-Veggie Chop Suey

1. Heat two servings each of the Filipino Turbo Chicken (page 138) (about two drumsticks per serving) and the Three-Veggie Chop Suey (page 152) in a skillet over medium-high heat for 3 minutes.

2. Divide the chicken and veggies between two plates.

Wonton Noodle Soup

1. Pour two servings of the Wonton Noodle Soup (page 140) in each of two bowls and microwave on high for 2 minutes; alternatively, combine the two servings in a small saucepan over medium-high heat for 3 minutes, or until it begins to simmer.

2. If you heated the soup on the stove, divide the soup between two bowls.

Cheeseburger Casserole, Shredded Kale and Pepita Pecan Salad

1. Plate two servings of the Shredded Kale and Pepita Pecan Salad (page 154).

2. Heat two servings of the Cheeseburger Casserole (page 142) in the microwave on high for 1 minute. Divide the casserole and place one serving on each of the plates with the salad.

Instant Pot Roast, Steak Rub, Jalapeño Cauliflower Mash, Pan-Roasted Garlic Oil

1. Heat two servings each of the Instant Pot Roast (page 146) and the Jalapeño Cauliflower Mash (page 156) in the microwave on high for 1½ minutes.

2. Divide the roast and mash between two plates and drizzle 1 tablespoon of the Pan-Roasted Garlic Oil (page 158) on top of the mash.

WEEK 4

Getting Started

Hooray for reaching week 4 of keto meal prepping! You have three weeks under your belt, so the recipes in this week will challenge you in the kitchen while giving you the most variety of all the meal plans. Each recipe is still easy to make, and you'll use a lot of the pantry essentials that you already have stocked in your kitchen. You'll be cooking the majority of the recipes on the stove, some in the oven, and one in the Instant Pot.

Print the downloadable week 4 PDF from **easyketomealprep.com/week4.**

What's on the Menu

If you need to adjust the quantities of the recipes for your needs, see the table on page 33 in the "What's on the Menu" section in the Introduction for more information.

MAIN DISHES

Blender Pancakes

COOKING METHOD: (skillet)
PREP TIME: 2 minutes
COOK TIME: 54 minutes
SERVES 6

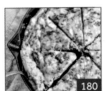
Loaded Breakfast Frittata

COOKING METHOD: (skillet, oven)
PREP TIME: 5 minutes
COOK TIME: 28 minutes
SERVES 4

Five-Spice Meatballs

COOKING METHOD: (oven)
PREP TIME: 5 minutes
COOK TIME: 20 minutes
SERVES 4

Chicken Korma

COOKING METHOD: (skillet)
PREP TIME: 10 minutes
COOK TIME: 20 minutes
SERVES 4

Instant Pot Beef Barbacoa

COOKING METHOD: (instant pot)
PREP TIME: 5 minutes
COOK TIME: 1 hour 40 minutes
SERVES 8

Easiest Lasagna

COOKING METHOD: (skillet, oven)
PREP TIME: 5 minutes
COOK TIME: 1 hour 3 minutes
SERVES 8

Black Pepper Chicken

COOKING METHOD: (skillet)
PREP TIME: 5 minutes
COOK TIME: 7 minutes
SERVES 4

save half for later

The recipes for the Instant Pot Beef Barbacoa (page 186) and the Easiest Lasagna (page 188) make 8 servings each, so you can freeze half of each to eat later. Instructions for freezing and reheating from frozen are in each recipe.

jenny's meal prep tip

Reward Yourself

Whether you've cooked up a storm or prepped just a couple of dishes, pat yourself on the back for a job well done because you've saved yourself some time during the week. Don't forget to reward yourself with a glass of wine (keto-friendly, of course), a bit of dark chocolate, a 30-minute nap in the afternoon, or whatever you feel you deserve!

SIDES

Shrimp Fried Rice 192

COOKING METHOD: 🍳
PREP TIME: 5 minutes
COOK TIME: 13 minutes
SERVES 4

Lo Mein 194

COOKING METHOD: 🍳
PREP TIME: 3 minutes
COOK TIME: 7 minutes
SERVES 4

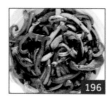

Classic Veggie Fajitas 196

COOKING METHOD: 🍳
PREP TIME: 5 minutes
COOK TIME: 12 minutes
SERVES 4

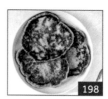

Garlic Naan 198

COOKING METHOD: 🍳
PREP TIME: 7 minutes
COOK TIME: 16 minutes
SERVES 4

Oven-Baked Bacon 200

COOKING METHOD: 🍳
PREP TIME: 1 minute
COOK TIME: 30 minutes
SERVES 6

CONDIMENTS AND GARNISHES

Tomato Avocado Salad 202

COOKING METHOD: —
PREP TIME: 10 minutes
COOK TIME: —
SERVES 4

Tangy Onion and Jalapeño Relish 204

COOKING METHOD: —
PREP TIME: 10 minutes
COOK TIME: —
YIELD: 1 to 1½ cups

Aji Verde Sauce 206

COOKING METHOD: —
PREP TIME: 5 minutes
COOK TIME: —
YIELD: ½ cup

Chili Garlic Paste 208

COOKING METHOD: 🍳
PREP TIME: 15 minutes
COOK TIME: 10 minutes
YIELD: ¾ cup

Ghee 210

COOKING METHOD: 🍳
PREP TIME: 1 minute
COOK TIME: 20 minutes
YIELD: 2 cups

Mayonnaise 212

COOKING METHOD: —
PREP TIME: 3 minutes
COOK TIME: —
YIELD: ¾ cup

Strawberries

Blueberries

Meal Plan

Cook Once a Week

DAY	BREAKFAST	LUNCH	DINNER
1	Blender Pancakes with Ghee, Oven-Baked Bacon, strawberries, blueberries	Easiest Lasagna	Five-Spice Meatballs, Chili Garlic Paste, Shrimp Fried Rice
2	Loaded Breakfast Frittata, Tomato Avocado Salad	Instant Pot Beef Barbacoa, Classic Veggie Fajitas, Tangy Onion and Jalapeño Relish, Aji Verde Sauce	Chicken Korma, Garlic Naan
3	Loaded Breakfast Frittata, Tomato Avocado Salad	Five-Spice Meatballs, Chili Garlic Paste, Shrimp Fried Rice	Black Pepper Chicken, Lo Mein
4	Blender Pancakes with Ghee, Oven-Baked Bacon, strawberries, blueberries	Easiest Lasagna	Instant Pot Beef Barbacoa, Classic Veggie Fajitas, Tangy Onion and Jalapeño Relish, Aji Verde Sauce
5	Blender Pancakes with Ghee, Oven-Baked Bacon, strawberries, blueberries	Black Pepper Chicken, Lo Mein	Chicken Korma, Garlic Naan
6	Free Meal	Leftovers	Leftovers
7	Free Meal	Leftovers	Leftovers

Cook Twice a Week

DAY	BREAKFAST	LUNCH	DINNER
1	Blender Pancakes with Ghee, Oven-Baked Bacon, strawberries, blueberries	Instant Pot Beef Barbacoa, Classic Veggie Fajitas, Tangy Onion and Jalapeño Relish, Aji Verde Sauce	Five-Spice Meatballs, Chili Garlic Paste, Shrimp Fried Rice
2	Blender Pancakes with Ghee, Oven-Baked Bacon, strawberries, blueberries	Five-Spice Meatballs, Chili Garlic Paste, Shrimp Fried Rice	Instant Pot Beef Barbacoa, Classic Veggie Fajitas, Tangy Onion and Jalapeño Relish, Aji Verde Sauce
3	Blender Pancakes with Ghee, Oven-Baked Bacon, strawberries, blueberries	Chicken Korma, Garlic Naan	Black Pepper Chicken, Lo Mein
4	Loaded Breakfast Frittata, Tomato Avocado Salad	Easiest Lasagna	Chicken Korma, Garlic Naan
5	Loaded Breakfast Frittata, Tomato Avocado Salad	Black Pepper Chicken, Lo Mein	Easiest Lasagna
6	Free Meal	Leftovers	Leftovers
7	Free Meal	Leftovers	Leftovers

Grocery List

In Your Pantry

Apple cider vinegar, 3 tablespoons plus 1 teaspoon

Avocado oil, 1¾ cups

Bay leaves, 3

Black pepper, 2 tablespoons plus ¼ teaspoon

Coconut aminos, ¾ cup

Coconut milk, full-fat, 2 (13½-ounce) cans

Garlic powder, 1½ tablespoons

Ground cumin, 1 tablespoon plus ½ teaspoon

Ground dried oregano, 1 tablespoon plus 1½ teaspoons

Olive oil, 2 tablespoons

Onion powder, 1 teaspoon

Red pepper flakes, 1 tablespoon

Sea salt, 3 tablespoons

Toasted sesame oil, ¼ cup

*Do you need to replenish any pantry items this week? Add them to your grocery list. You can print the downloadable list from **easyketomealprep.com/pantry** to take with you to the grocery store. Check off all the items under the In Your Pantry category because these are already on the Pantry Essentials list.*

Other Items

Baking powder, 2½ teaspoons

Black pepper, cracked, 2 teaspoons

Blanched almond flour, 1 cup

Coconut flour, ½ cup plus 1 tablespoon

Coconut cream, 1 (5.4-ounce) can

Marinara sauce, 2 (18-ounce) jars

Psyllium husks, 2½ tablespoons

Shirataki noodles, 2 (8-ounce) packages

Tomato paste, 4½ tablespoons

Unsweetened shredded coconut, ½ cup

Vanilla extract, 1 tablespoon

Special Equipment

Nut milk bag

Meat and Seafood

Bacon, 1 pound

Beef, boneless chuck roast, 2½ pounds

Beef, ground, 2 pounds

Chicken thighs, boneless, skinless, 2 pounds

Pork, ground, 1 pound

Shrimp, raw, large, 1 pound

Condiments and Spices

Black peppercorns, whole, 2 teaspoons

Chipotle powder, 2 teaspoons

Dijon mustard, ½ teaspoon

Five-spice powder, 1½ teaspoons

Garam masala, 2 teaspoons

Turmeric powder, 2 teaspoons

White pepper, ground, ½ teaspoon

Use the prepared Chili Oil (page 116) from week 2 instead of making a batch of Chili Garlic Paste (page 208).

Frozen Items

Riced cauliflower, 2 (12-ounce) bags

Produce

Asparagus, 1 bunch

Bell peppers, 3 red, 2 green, 1 yellow

Chives, 1 bunch

Cilantro, 3 bunches

Cucumber, 1 small

Garlic, 56 cloves (about 5½ bulbs)

Ginger, 1 (8-inch) piece

Green chard, 1 bunch

Green onions, 1 bunch

Hass avocado, 1 medium

Lemons, 3

Limes, 3

Jalapeño peppers, 3

Onions, red, 1 small, 1 medium

Onions, yellow, 4 small

Spinach, 1 bunch

Tomatoes, cherry, 10 ounces

Eggs and Dairy

Eggs, large, 16

Butter, unsalted, 2 cups (4 sticks)

Feta cheese, 8 ounces

Goat cheese, 8 ounces

Mozzarella cheese, 1 pound

Ricotta cheese, 1 pound

Substitute 1 pound of almond milk cream cheese or lactose-free cream cheese for the ricotta cheese and 1 pound of crumbled fresh goat cheese for the mozzarella.

Swap the 4 sticks of butter for an 8-ounce jar of ready-to-use ghee.

Meal Prep Game Plan

ESTIMATED TIME SPENT: 15 minutes

1. Read and review the week's menu, grocery list, meal plan, and recipes. Print the downloadable PDF for the week.

   If you want to include keto-friendly snacks or treats to your meal plan for the week, add the ingredients you need to the Other Items category of your grocery list. Some ideas for this week are Parmesan Crisps Three Ways (page 250), Peanut Butter Cookies (page 272), and Coconut Butter Bites (page 286).

2. Review the In Your Pantry section of the grocery list and check off any items that you already have on hand. Be sure you have enough of each pantry item for the recipes you will prepare on meal prep day.

3. Review the Prep Time-Savers, Substitutions, and Dairy Options sections of the grocery list.

   You can buy the convenience items suggested to help cut your prep time this week. Cross off the ingredients that each convenience item replaces on the grocery list.

   Mark ingredients that you need to substitute for; also take note of your preferred dairy option and indicate your choice.

4. Check your calendar for family/work/social events in the coming week. Mark any meals when you won't be eating your prepared dishes. Swap these meals with Leftovers or a Free Meal.

ESTIMATED TIME SPENT: 45 minutes

Shop for groceries. Don't forget your printed grocery list (and Pantry Essentials list if you're shopping for both).

ESTIMATED TIME SPENT: 1 hour

POWER HOUR PREP

1. Prepare the following condiments if you decide not to buy the premade versions:

   - Ghee (page 210)
   - Mayonnaise (page 212)

2. You will use a lot of aromatics and herbs this week. Store each one separately in a zip-top plastic bag or airtight glass container in the refrigerator:

   - Mince 54 cloves of garlic (about 1 cup, 2 tablespoons, and 2 teaspoons).

   To make shorter work of mincing this large amount of garlic, place the peeled garlic cloves in a food processor and pulse for 5 seconds. Scrape the sides of the bowl and puree for another 5 seconds until the garlic resembles a minced texture.

3. Peel and grate 8 inches of ginger (about ¼ cup).

   - Slice 1 small yellow onion, chop 1 small yellow onion and 1 red onion, and cut 1 small yellow onion into 8 wedges.
   - Thinly slice ¾ cup of green onions.
   - Chop ¼ cup of chives.
   - Chop 2 bunches of cilantro.

Cook Once a Week

For your fourth week of meal prepping, you will prepare a lot of the recipes on the stove, and you can easily cook multiple dishes at the same time.

> *Cool each cooked dish for 10 to 15 minutes before transferring to the containers specified in the* 🄰 *Refrigerate This section of the recipes.*

MEAL PREP DAY

1	Arrange two racks in the middle of the oven. Prepare the Oven-Baked Bacon (page 200). Place the baking sheets in the cold oven and set the temperature to 400°F.
2	While the bacon is in the oven, cook the Instant Pot Beef Barbacoa (page 186) in the Instant Pot.
3	Simmer the sauce for the Easiest Lasagna (page 188) on the stove, assemble the lasagna in the casserole dish, and set it aside.
	The Oven-Baked Bacon should be done at this point, so take it out of the oven and let it cool for 2 minutes before pouring the bacon fat into a small bowl. You will use the fat for the Loaded Breakfast Frittata and the Shrimp Fried Rice.
	Reduce the oven temperature to 375°F.
4	Prepare the Loaded Breakfast Frittata (page 180) on the stove. Move the pan to the top rack in the oven and bake.
	Bake the Easiest Lasagna on the bottom rack at the same time as the frittata.
5	Cook the Chicken Korma (page 184) on the stove.
6	Cook the Blender Pancakes (page 178) while the Chicken Korma is simmering.
	The frittata should be cooked at this point. Remove it from the oven.
7	Cook the Garlic Naan (page 198) in the same pan used for the Blender Pancakes.
8	Cook the Shrimp Fried Rice (page 192) on the stove.
	The Easiest Lasagna should be done baking. Remove it from the oven and increase the oven temperature to 400°F.

9	Prepare the Five-Spice Meatballs (page 182) and bake them in the oven.
10	Cook the Classic Veggie Fajitas (page 196) on the stove.
11	Cook the Black Pepper Chicken (page 190) on the stove. Remove the meatballs from the oven.
12	Cook the Lo Mein (page 194) on the stove.
13	Prepare the Chili Garlic Paste (page 208) on the stove.
14	Prepare the Tomato Avocado Salad (page 202). Refrigerate immediately.
15	Prepare the Tangy Onion and Jalapeño Relish (page 204). Refrigerate immediately.
16	Prepare the Aji Verde Sauce (page 206). Refrigerate immediately.
17	Rinse the berries and dry them thoroughly with paper towels. Store in the refrigerator until ready to eat.

MEAL PREP DAY 1: START OF THE WEEK

1	Arrange two racks in the middle of the oven. Prepare the Oven-Baked Bacon (page 200). Place the baking sheets in the cold oven and set the temperature to 400°F.
2	While the bacon is in the oven, cook the Instant Pot Beef Barbacoa (page 186) in the Instant Pot.
3	Cook the Chicken Korma (page 184) on the stove. The Oven-Baked Bacon should be done at this point, so take it out of the oven and let it cool for 2 minutes before pouring the bacon fat into a small bowl. You will use the fat with the Loaded Breakfast Frittata and the Shrimp Fried Rice.
4	Prepare the Five-Spice Meatballs (page 182) and bake them at 400°F.
5	Cook the Blender Pancakes (page 178) on the stove while the Chicken Korma is simmering.
6	Cook the Garlic Naan (page 198) in the same pan used for the Blender Pancakes. Remove the meatballs from the oven.
7	Cook the Shrimp Fried Rice (page 192) on the stove.
8	Cook the Classic Veggie Fajitas (page 196) on the stove.
9	Prepare the Chili Garlic Paste (page 208) on the stove.
10	Prepare the Tangy Onion and Jalapeño Relish (page 204). Refrigerate immediately.
11	Prepare the Aji Verde Sauce (page 206). Refrigerate immediately.
12	Rinse the berries and dry thoroughly with paper towels. Store in the refrigerator until ready to eat.

MEAL PREP DAY 2: MIDWEEK

1	Arrange two racks in the middle of the oven and preheat the oven to 375°F.
	Simmer the sauce for the Easiest Lasagna (page 188) on the stove, assemble the lasagna in the casserole dish, and set it aside.
2	Prepare the Loaded Breakfast Frittata (page 180) on the stove. Move the pan to the top rack of the oven and bake.
	Bake the Easiest Lasagna on the bottom rack at the same time as the frittata.
3	Cook the Black Pepper Chicken (page 190) on the stove.
	The frittata should be cooked at this point. Remove it from the oven.
4	Cook the Lo Mein (page 194) on the stove.
5	Prepare the Tomato Avocado Salad (page 202). Refrigerate immediately.
	The Easiest Lasagna should be done baking. Remove it from the oven.

My Week 4 Meal Prep Notes

Blender Pancakes

SERVES 6, 4 pancakes per serving • **PREP TIME:** 2 minutes
COOK TIME: 54 minutes

Sometimes while I'm eating keto, I crave anything that has a breadlike texture, so I came up with these Blender Pancakes that totally hit the spot. You can prepare the batter in a couple of minutes by blitzing all the ingredients in the blender until smooth. Make sure to cook the pancakes over low heat to prevent the goat cheese from bubbling too much and burning quickly. Low and slow is the key to making these pancakes!

1 cup (about 8 ounces) fresh goat cheese, softened

1 cup blanched almond flour

4 large eggs

¼ cup Ghee (page 210), softened, plus 3 tablespoons for frying

1 tablespoon vanilla extract

1 teaspoon baking powder

1. Place all the ingredients in a blender except the ghee for frying. Blend until smooth.

2. Preheat a large cast-iron pan over low heat. Lightly oil the pan with 1 teaspoon of ghee.

3. Slowly pour 3 tablespoons of the batter into the pan for a pancake that's 3 inches in diameter. Cook four pancakes at a time.

4. Cook for 4 to 5 minutes on the first side. Once the pancakes start bubbling, flip them and cook on the other side for 3 to 4 minutes, until golden brown.

5. Transfer the cooked pancakes to a glass container and repeat steps 2 through 4 with the remaining batter, adding another teaspoon of ghee to the pan before cooking each batch.

Once the pancakes are cool, cover the container and store in the refrigerator for up to 5 days.

Stack the pancakes in a zip-top freezer bag with pieces of parchment paper between them to prevent the pancakes from sticking together. Gently squeeze the bag to remove any excess air before sealing. Store in the freezer for up to 2 months.

Grab the number of pancakes you want to eat. Reheat from frozen in a toaster oven at 375°F for 5 minutes.

Approximate macros per serving:
Calories: **228** • Fat: **22g** • Protein: **6g** • Net Carbs: **1g** • Fiber: **1g**

Loaded Breakfast Frittata

SERVES 4, 2 slices per serving • **PREP TIME:** 5 minutes
COOK TIME: 28 minutes

Let the frittata cool before slicing into 8 wedges. Transfer to a glass container, cover, and store in the refrigerator for up to 5 days.

There are dozens of combinations for putting together a frittata. More often than not, I use any leftover veggies that I can find in the refrigerator, so I don't end up throwing anything away. My rule of thumb is to add bacon, cheese, and aromatics to the veggies to make the frittata super tasty. This is a good basic recipe to start with. It's perfect as a make-ahead meal that has a ton of flavor because it's loaded with bell peppers, spinach, and feta. You'll enjoy eating this frittata for breakfast or pretty much any meal of the day!

8 large eggs

¼ cup full-fat coconut milk

1 teaspoon sea salt

1 teaspoon black pepper

½ teaspoon ground dried oregano

2 tablespoons bacon fat from Oven-Baked Bacon (page 200)

1 small onion, chopped

4 cloves garlic, minced (about 4 teaspoons)

1 red bell pepper, chopped

1 bunch fresh spinach (about 4 cups), stems removed

1 cup crumbled feta cheese

2 tablespoons chopped fresh chives

1. Preheat the oven to 375°F.

2. Whisk the eggs, coconut milk, salt, pepper, and oregano in a large bowl until frothy.

3. Preheat a cast-iron pan over medium-high heat.

4. Melt the bacon fat in the hot pan for a few seconds.

5. Add the onion and garlic. Sauté for 2 minutes, until the onion begins to soften and become translucent.

6. Mix in the bell pepper and sauté for 5 minutes, until soft.

7. Pile on the spinach and sauté for 1 minute, until wilted.

8. Once the vegetables are cooked, slowly pour the egg mixture into the pan. Gently swirl the eggs to distribute them evenly.

9. Sprinkle the feta cheese and chives on top. Move the pan to the oven and bake for 18 to 20 minutes, until the eggs are set.

Approximate macros per serving: —————————————
Calories: **360** • Fat: **26g** • Protein: **21g** • Net Carbs: **10g** • Fiber: **3g**

Five-Spice Meatballs

SERVES 4 • **PREP TIME:** 5 minutes • **COOK TIME:** 20 minutes

The aroma of five-spice powder brings back memories of my childhood when my family would head to Chinatown to grab our holiday ham for celebrating the New Year. We would always stop to eat at a wonton restaurant, and that restaurant served the best Chinese meatballs ever. That memory inspired me to make these Five-Spice Meatballs that highlight the flavor of good-quality pork without any additives or fillers. Just a few simple ingredients are all it takes to create these savory and juicy morsels.

Transfer the meatballs to a glass container, cover, and store in the refrigerator for up to 5 days.

Transfer the meatballs to a zip-top freezer bag and gently squeeze to remove any excess air before sealing. Store in the freezer for up to 2 months.

Defrost by submerging the bag of frozen meatballs in a deep bowl filled with cold water; place the bowl in the fridge for an hour, replacing the water after 30 minutes. Reheat the meatballs in a skillet over medium heat for 2 minutes.

1 pound ground pork

1 large egg

¼ cup thinly sliced green onions

2 tablespoons coconut aminos

1 tablespoon coconut flour

1 (1½-inch) piece ginger, peeled and grated (about ¾ tablespoon)

3 cloves garlic, minced (about 3 teaspoons)

1½ teaspoons five-spice powder

¾ teaspoon sea salt

½ teaspoon ground white pepper

1. Preheat the oven to 400°F. Line a rimmed baking sheet with parchment paper.

2. Place all the ingredients in a large bowl and mix well with your hands.

3. Form the pork mixture into 1½-inch meatballs, about 1 ounce each. Arrange the meatballs evenly on the prepared baking sheet.

4. Bake for 20 minutes, until the meatballs are cooked through and the internal temperature is 160°F.

Approximate macros per serving: ───────────
Calories: **301** • Fat: **22g** • Protein: **21g** • Net Carbs: **3g** • Fiber: **1g**

Chicken Korma

SERVES 4 • **PREP TIME:** 10 minutes • **COOK TIME:** 20 minutes

 Transfer the chicken with the sauce to a glass container, cover, and store in the refrigerator for up to 5 days.

Transfer the chicken with the sauce to a zip-top freezer bag and gently press to remove any excess air before sealing. Store in the freezer for up to 2 months.

Remove the frozen chicken and sauce from the zip-top bag and place it in a medium saucepan over medium heat. Let it thaw for 8 to 10 minutes. Use a wooden spoon to break the Chicken Korma into smaller pieces to heat it more quickly. Once it's no longer frozen, let it simmer for 5 minutes.

The first time I had chicken korma, Will had made it for my birthday dinner using a jarred simmer sauce. He served it with yellow rice. It was so good that we kept the pantry stocked with jars of that sauce. Although the jarred sauce was convenient, I wanted to make a homemade version so I could use coconut milk instead of heavy cream and adjust the spices according to my preference. This one-pot meal has a good amount of creamy sauce; the Garlic Naan (page 198) is perfect for dipping in the sauce. The ingredient list may seem daunting, but it's mostly spices, basic ingredients, and pantry staples that you just measure and mix together in the pot. Then you simmer it until the chicken and veggies are cooked.

2 tablespoons Ghee (page 210)

1 small onion, chopped

4 cloves garlic, minced (about 2 teaspoons)

1 (2-inch) piece ginger, peeled and grated (about 1 tablespoon)

1 pound boneless, skinless chicken thighs, cut into 1-inch pieces

1½ teaspoons sea salt

¼ teaspoon black pepper

1½ tablespoons tomato paste

2 teaspoons turmeric powder

2 teaspoons garam masala

½ teaspoon ground cumin

½ (13½-ounce) can full-fat coconut milk (about ¾ cup plus 1 tablespoon)

1 (5.4-ounce) can coconut cream

½ cup unsweetened shredded coconut

Juice of 1 lemon (about 2 tablespoons)

1 red bell pepper, cut into 8 slices

1 green bell pepper, cut into 8 slices

¼ cup chopped fresh cilantro

1. Heat a medium saucepan over medium heat. Melt the ghee for a few seconds.

2. Add the onion, garlic, and ginger. Sauté for 5 minutes, until the mixture is fragrant and the onion begins to soften.

3. Season the chicken with the salt and pepper and add it to the saucepan. Sauté until slightly cooked, about 2 minutes.

4. Add the tomato paste, turmeric, garam masala, and cumin. Stir and sauté for 1 minute.

Approximate macros per serving: ——————
Calories: **466** • Fat: **33g** • Protein: **26g** • Net Carbs: **14g** • Fiber: **5g**

5. Pour in the coconut milk and coconut cream and then add the shredded coconut and lemon juice. Mix well and bring to a boil. Reduce the heat to medium-low and let it simmer for 5 to 8 minutes, until slightly thickened.

6. Add the red and green bell peppers and adjust the salt to taste. Mix and continue simmering for 5 minutes.

7. Turn off the heat and mix in the chopped cilantro.

Instant Pot Beef Barbacoa

SERVES 8 • **PREP TIME:** 5 minutes, plus 30 minutes to allow the roast to rest • **COOK TIME:** 1 hour 40 minutes, plus 25 minutes of natural pressure release

Tasty, flavorful meat that doesn't take a lot of prep work is always a winner in my book. Searing a nice piece of chuck roast and then generously seasoning it before cooking it on high pressure will give you fork-tender beef that is incredibly versatile. Pair this barbacoa with the Classic Veggie Fajitas (page 196) plus a dollop of the Aji Verde Sauce (page 206), or use it as an omelet filling for a quick breakfast!

Transfer one half of the beef and the cooking juices into a glass container. Cover and store in the refrigerator for up to 5 days.

Transfer the second half of the beef and the cooking juices to a zip-top freezer bag. Gently press to remove any excess air before sealing. Store in the freezer for up to 2 months.

Move the bag to the refrigerator and let it thaw overnight. Reheat the beef and the juices in a medium saucepan over medium heat for 5 to 8 minutes.

Jenny's tips

Place the beef in a stand mixer fitted with a flat beater attachment. Turn it on medium-low speed for 10 seconds to shred the beef.

No Instant Pot? Sear the beef on the stove and transfer it to a slow cooker. Cook on the low setting for 8 to 10 hours.

2½ pounds boneless beef chuck roast

2 teaspoons sea salt

2 teaspoons black pepper

1 tablespoon Ghee (page 210)

10 cloves garlic, minced (about 3 tablespoons plus 1 teaspoon)

2 teaspoons whole black peppercorns

3 bay leaves

1 tablespoon ground cumin

1 tablespoon ground dried oregano

2 teaspoons chipotle powder

½ cup water

Juice of 2 limes (about ¼ cup)

1. Remove the beef from the refrigerator and let it sit at room temperature for 20 minutes. Blot both sides with a paper towel to remove any excess moisture to help it sear nicely. Season both sides with the salt and pepper.

2. Press the Sauté button on the Instant Pot and select High heat. Let it heat up for 1 minute.

3. Melt the ghee for a few seconds.

4. Place the beef in the Instant Pot and sear the first side for 5 minutes.

5. Flip and sear the second side for another 5 minutes.

6. Immediately press the Off or Cancel button.

7. Arrange the garlic, peppercorns, and bay leaves around the beef and season the meat with the cumin, oregano, and chipotle powder. Add the water and lime juice.

8. Cover and make sure the vent valve is in the sealed position. Press the Meat/Stew button and set the timer for 90 minutes.

Approximate macros per serving:
Calories: **221** • Fat: **11g** • Protein: **31g** • Net Carbs: **2g** • Fiber: **1g**

9. Let the pressure release naturally, about 25 minutes. Slowly releasing the pressure allows the meat to cook a little bit more while the temperature in the pot decreases. Remove the lid and let the beef cool for 10 minutes. Then shred it with two forks.

10. Divide the beef and cooking juices into two portions—one for the refrigerator and the other for the freezer.

Easiest Lasagna

SERVES 8 • **PREP TIME:** 5 minutes • **COOK TIME:** 1 hour 3 minutes

This noodle-free lasagna is made possible by substituting nutrient-dense leafy green chard for the lasagna noodles! Making lasagna has always intimidated me because it involves a million and one steps, so I simplified it to be meal prep friendly. Even if you make this lasagna dairy-free, the result is a decadent and comforting dish that the whole family will love.

1 tablespoon avocado oil

2 pounds ground beef

2 (18-ounce) jars marinara sauce

1 tablespoon garlic powder

2 teaspoons sea salt

2 teaspoons black pepper

2 large eggs

1 pound ricotta cheese

1 bunch green chard, stems removed, cut into strips

1 pound mozzarella cheese, shredded

1. Heat a large saucepan over medium-high heat.

2. Pour in the avocado oil and add the ground beef. Sauté until no longer pink, about 8 minutes. Use a wooden spoon to break down big chunks of the beef so it cooks evenly.

3. Pour the marinara sauce into the pan and season with the garlic powder, salt, and pepper. Stir and bring to a boil. Reduce the heat to medium and let simmer for 20 minutes.

4. Preheat the oven to 375°F.

5. In a medium-sized bowl, stir together the eggs and ricotta cheese.

6. Grab a lasagna pan or a 11 by 7-inch casserole dish. Scoop one-third of the meat sauce into the pan and spread it evenly across the bottom.

7. Lay the chard leaves side by side on top of the sauce.

8. Spoon one-third of the ricotta cheese mixture on top of the chard leaves and spread it evenly with a spatula.

9. Sprinkle a handful of mozzarella cheese on top of the ricotta cheese mixture.

10. Repeat steps 6 through 9 two more times to create a total of three layers of the meat sauce, chard leaves, ricotta mixture, and mozzarella. Top with some more mozzarella.

Substitute almond milk cream cheese or lactose-free cream cheese for the ricotta cheese and crumbled fresh goat cheese for the mozzarella.

Slice one half of the lasagna into 4 servings and transfer to a glass container. Cover and store in the refrigerator for up to 5 days.

Wrap the other half of the lasagna with plastic wrap. Place it in a zip-top freezer bag and remove any excess air before sealing. Store in the freezer for up to 1 month.

Move the bag of lasagna to the refrigerator to thaw overnight. Preheat the oven to 375°F. Carefully remove the plastic wrap from the lasagna and place it on a baking dish. Heat it in the oven for 8 minutes, until the cheese is melted.

Approximate macros per serving: ———
Calories: **571** • Fat: **36g** • Protein: **46g** • Net Carbs: **11g** • Fiber: **3g**

11. Bake for 30 to 35 minutes, until the cheese is bubbly.

12. Let cool for 15 minutes. Then cut the lasagna into two halves—one for the refrigerator and the other for the freezer.

Black Pepper Chicken

SERVES 4 • **PREP TIME:** 10 minutes • **COOK TIME:** 7 minutes

Transfer the chicken to a glass container. Cover and store in the refrigerator for up to 5 days.

This stir-fry chicken is a super quick and easy dish that is ready in less than 20 minutes! Marinating it for a few minutes infuses the chicken pieces with umami goodness, and adding a little bit of cilantro at the end completes this simple meal.

1 pound boneless, skinless chicken thighs, cut into 1-inch pieces

4 tablespoons coconut aminos

1 tablespoon plus 2 teaspoons toasted sesame oil, divided

2 teaspoons cracked black pepper

1 tablespoon avocado oil

1 bunch asparagus, sliced into 2-inch pieces

1 small onion, cut into 8 wedges

¼ cup chopped fresh cilantro

1. Place the chicken in a medium-sized bowl and season it with 2 tablespoons of the coconut aminos, 1 tablespoon of the toasted sesame oil, and the pepper. Mix and set aside to marinate for 5 minutes.

2. Heat a large cast-iron pan over high heat.

3. Pour in the avocado oil and add the chicken. Sauté for 5 minutes, until golden brown. Transfer to a plate and set aside.

4. Place the asparagus and onion in the same pan and sauté for 2 minutes.

5. Season the veggies with the remaining 2 tablespoons of the coconut aminos. Stir and return the cooked chicken to the pan.

6. Turn off the heat. Drizzle the remaining toasted sesame oil on top and mix well. Top with the cilantro.

Approximate macros per serving: ————————
Calories: **253** • Fat: **14g** • Protein: **26g** • Net Carbs: **5g** • Fiber: **0g**

Shrimp Fried Rice

SERVES 4 • **PREP TIME:** 5 minutes • **COOK TIME:** 13 minutes

Transfer the rice to a glass container, cover, and store in the refrigerator for up to 4 days.

It's hard to tell that this fried rice is made with riced cauliflower instead of regular jasmine rice because of the different layers of flavors that hit your palate with the first forkful. A quick sauté in bacon fat with garlic and onion yields tender and juicy shrimp that's not rubbery. Tossing the cooked fried rice with sesame oil at the end gives it a toasty finish.

Jenny's tip

Place the bags of cauliflower rice in the refrigerator overnight so they're ready to go the next day.

2 tablespoons bacon fat from the Oven-Baked Bacon (200)

½ small onion, sliced

2 cloves garlic, minced (about 2 teaspoons)

1 pound large raw shrimp, peeled and deveined, each shrimp chopped into 3 pieces

2 (12-ounce) bags frozen riced cauliflower, thawed

2 tablespoons coconut aminos

1½ tablespoons toasted sesame oil

¼ cup chopped fresh chives

1. Heat a large cast-iron pan over high heat.

2. Melt the bacon fat, then add the onion and garlic. Sauté for 1 minute, until the garlic begins to brown.

3. Toss in the shrimp and cook until pink, about 3 minutes. Immediately transfer to a small bowl and set aside.

4. In the same pan over high heat, cook the riced cauliflower, stirring occasionally, for 7 to 8 minutes. Any excess water from the cauliflower will evaporate during cooking, and after 8 minutes, the cauliflower should have a drier consistency. All the bits of onion and garlic that were left at the bottom of the pan will blend in nicely with the cauliflower rice to give it added flavor.

5. Season the cauliflower rice with the coconut aminos and return the cooked shrimp, onion, and garlic to the pan. Sauté for 1 more minute.

6. Turn off the heat, season with the sesame oil, and mix well. Sprinkle the chives on top.

Approximate macros per serving:
Calories: **240** • Fat: **13g** • Protein: **20g** • Net Carbs: **7g** • Fiber: **5g**

Lo Mein

SERVES 4 • **PREP TIME:** 3 minutes • **COOK TIME:** 7 minutes

Low-carb lo mein, oh yeah! The secret ingredient? Japanese shirataki noodles made from konjac root. The noodles are almost calorie-free and carbohydrate-free, making them the perfect substitute for regular noodles.

 Transfer the noodles to a glass container. Cover and refrigerate for up to 5 days.

Jenny's tip

Substitute 1 tablespoon of tamari for the coconut aminos if you prefer its flavor, which is more similar to regular soy sauce.

2 (8-ounce) packages shirataki noodles

2 tablespoons coconut aminos

2 teaspoons toasted sesame oil

2 teaspoons Ghee (page 210)

½ small onion, thinly sliced

3 cloves garlic, minced (about 3 teaspoons)

1 teaspoon black pepper

¼ cup thinly sliced green onions

1. Place the shirataki noodles in a mesh strainer and drain the packing liquid. Rinse the noodles well in cold water until they feel squeaky clean. Drain the noodles well.

2. Transfer the noodles to a medium-sized bowl. Season with the coconut aminos and sesame oil. Mix well and let sit for 5 minutes.

3. Heat a cast-iron pan over medium-high heat.

4. Melt the ghee for a few seconds.

5. Add the onion and garlic. Sauté for 2 minutes, until the onion begins to soften.

6. Pour the shirataki noodles and the marinade into the pan.

7. Sauté for 5 minutes.

8. Turn off the heat. Season with the pepper and add the green onions. Mix to combine.

Approximate macros per serving: ———————
Calories: **73** • Fat: **5g** • Protein: **1g** • Net Carbs: **1g** • Fiber: **4g**

Classic Veggie Fajitas

SERVES 4 • **PREP TIME:** 5 minutes • **COOK TIME:** 12 minutes

Transfer the fajitas to a glass container, cover, and store in the refrigerator for up to 5 days.

I like to load up my plate with a big serving of veggies when I'm making a taco bowl because it tastes so much better than plain rice or beans. Mixing colored bell peppers with a red onion makes these Classic Veggie Fajitas visually appealing as well!

1 tablespoon avocado oil

1 red bell pepper, sliced

1 yellow bell pepper, sliced

1 green bell pepper, sliced

1 medium red onion, sliced

1 teaspoon ground dried oregano

Sea salt to taste

1. Heat a large cast-iron pan over high heat.

2. Pour in the avocado oil and place all the bell peppers and red onion in the pan. Sauté for 2 minutes.

3. Season with the oregano and salt and continue sautéing for 8 to 10 minutes, until the vegetables are tender.

Approximate macros per serving:
Calories: **75** • Fat: **4g** • Protein: **2g** • Net Carbs: **7g** • Fiber: **3g**

Garlic Naan

Once cool, cut each naan into 4 pieces to make it easier to pack and eat. Transfer it to a glass container, cover, and store in the refrigerator for up to 5 days.

SERVES 4, 1 naan per serving • **PREP TIME:** 7 minutes
COOK TIME: 16 minutes

A keto-friendly bread? You got that right! I had to experiment with a couple of bags of coconut flour before I nailed down the ingredient ratio so that the consistency is just right. Psyllium husks are a great binder in the absence of regular flour, and it makes this naan light and fluffy.

½ cup coconut flour

2 ½ tablespoons psyllium husks

1 ½ teaspoons baking powder

1 teaspoon garlic powder

1 teaspoon onion powder

1 cup full-fat coconut milk

4 tablespoons ghee, divided, for the pan

1. In a medium-sized bowl, combine the coconut flour, psyllium husks, baking powder, garlic powder, and onion powder. Mix well. Pour in the coconut milk and mix until a dough forms.

2. Divide the dough into 4 equal portions and roll into balls. Let the divided dough rest for 5 minutes.

3. Cut 2 pieces of parchment paper, each 8 inches long.

4. Place one parchment sheet on a cutting board and place one ball of dough on top of the parchment. Cover the dough with the second piece of parchment paper.

5. Using a rolling pin or large can, flatten the dough until it's about ¼ inch thick. Put the flattened dough on a plate and set aside. Repeat the same steps for the remaining pieces of dough.

6. Heat a cast-iron pan over medium heat. Melt 1 tablespoon of the ghee and place a ball of dough in the pan. Fry one naan at a time.

7. Pan-fry the naan until the first side is browned, about 2 minutes.

8. Flip and fry the other side for 2 more minutes. You'll know the naan is ready when it has puffed up and the edges are browned. Transfer the cooked naan to a plate.

9. Melt another tablespoon of ghee and fry the remaining pieces of dough.

Approximate macros per serving:
Calories: **307** • Fat: **27g** • Protein: **3g** • Net Carbs: **1g** • Fiber: **12g**

Oven-Baked Bacon

Cover the container and store in the refrigerator for up to 5 days.

SERVES 6, 3 slices per serving • **PREP TIME:** 1 minute
COOK TIME: 30 minutes

Cooking bacon in the oven is a foolproof method because you just set the timer and walk away until it's crispy all the way through. There's no need to flip it because it cooks evenly in the oven. Cleanup is also easier because you won't end up with bacon grease splattered all over your stove!

1 pound bacon (about 18 slices)

1. Line two rimmed baking sheets with foil. Arrange the bacon on the prepared baking sheets in a single layer. Make sure the pieces do not overlap.

2. Place the baking sheets in a cold oven and turn the temperature to 400°F. Bake for 20 minutes. The oven will be at the set cooking temperature halfway through baking.

3. Check the bacon and rotate the baking sheets if one side is cooking faster than the other. Swap the baking sheet on the top rack with the one on the bottom rack so the two trays bake evenly.

4. Bake for another 8 to 10 minutes, until crispy and golden brown.

5. Transfer the bacon to a glass container.

6. Cool the baking sheets with the bacon fat drippings before pouring the drippings into a small bowl to use for the Loaded Breakfast Frittata (page 180) and Shrimp Fried Rice (page 192).

Approximate macros per serving: ───────
Calories: **336** • Fat: **25g** • Protein: **25g** • Net Carbs: **0g** • Fiber: **0g**

Tomato Avocado Salad

SERVES 4, ¾ cup per serving • **PREP TIME:** 10 minutes
COOK TIME: —

Creamy avocado, fresh cucumber, and sweet tomatoes make a perfect snack. As a side for the Loaded Breakfast Frittata (page 180), it's part of a filling and satisfying meal.

1 (10-ounce) package cherry tomatoes, quartered

1 small cucumber, diced

1 medium Hass avocado, diced

2 tablespoons olive oil

Juice of 1 lemon (about 2 tablespoons)

½ teaspoon sea salt

In a small bowl, combine all the ingredients and mix well.

Transfer the salad to a glass container. Cover and store in the refrigerator for up to 3 days.

Jenny's tip

Remove the seeds from the cherry tomatoes to reduce the amount of liquid produced by the salad.

Approximate macros per serving:
Calories: **139** • Fat: **12g** • Protein: **1g** • Net Carbs: **5g** • Fiber: **3g**

Tangy Onion and Jalapeño Relish

YIELD: 1 to 1½ cups, ¼ cup per serving • **PREP TIME:** 10 minutes
COOK TIME: —

Transfer the relish to a jar. Cover and store in the refrigerator for up to 5 days.

One of my favorite toppings for the Crispy Carnitas (page 96) and the Instant Pot Beef Barbacoa (page 186) is a combination of onion, jalapeño peppers, and cilantro. It's bright and fresh, and it adds a little bit of a zing to a dish!

jenny's tip

If you want a spicier relish, do not remove the seeds from the jalapeño peppers.

1 bunch cilantro leaves, chopped

1 small red onion, chopped

2 jalapeño peppers, seeded and chopped

Juice of 1 lime (about 2 tablespoons)

¼ teaspoon sea salt

In a small bowl, combine all the ingredients and mix well.

Approximate macros per serving: —————————
Calories: **13** • Fat: **0g** • Protein: **0g** • Net Carbs: **3g** • Fiber: **0g**

Aji Verde Sauce

YIELD: ½ cup, 2 tablespoons per serving • **PREP TIME:** 5 minutes
COOK TIME: —

This green sauce tastes great slathered on meat and veggies or served as a dip for crudité. I first tried Aji Verde at a Peruvian joint I used to frequent, and after that first taste, I knew I had to make it at home. The owner was kind enough to share with me the key ingredients in this magical sauce, which is super easy to make!

¾ cup packed roughly chopped fresh cilantro leaves

¼ cup thinly sliced green onions

½ cup Mayonnaise (page 212)

1 jalapeño pepper, seeded and chopped

2 cloves garlic, peeled and smashed

1 teaspoon apple cider vinegar

Place all the ingredients in a food processor and puree until smooth.

 Transfer the sauce to a jar, cover, and store in the refrigerator for up to 1 week.

Jenny's tip

For a spicier sauce, do not remove the seeds from the jalapeño pepper.

Approximate macros per serving:
Calories: **93** • Fat: **10g** • Protein: **0g** • Net Carbs: **1g** • Fiber: **0g**

Chili Garlic Paste

YIELD: ¾ cup, 1 tablespoon per serving • **PREP TIME:** 15 minutes
COOK TIME: 10 minutes

 Transfer the Chili Garlic Paste to a jar. Cover and store in the refrigerator for up to 2 weeks.

I always have a jar of this Chili Garlic Paste ready in the refrigerator so I can use it in stir-fries, on grilled meat, and in just about anything else that needs a little heat and a pop of flavor. Using freshly minced garlic and freshly grated ginger makes a big difference; the quality and taste are so much better than ready-to-use jarred versions. Everything you need to make this is probably in your refrigerator and pantry!

½ cup avocado oil

24 cloves garlic, peeled and minced (about ½ cup)

1 (4½-inch) piece ginger, peeled and grated (about 2¼ tablespoons)

3 tablespoons tomato paste

1 tablespoon red pepper flakes

¼ cup coconut aminos

3 tablespoons apple cider vinegar

¼ teaspoon sea salt

1. Heat a skillet over medium-low heat.

2. Pour the avocado oil into the pan and add the garlic and ginger. Sauté for 1 minute until fragrant.

3. Mix the tomato paste and red pepper flakes with the garlic and ginger mixture. Simmer for 1 to 2 minutes.

4. Add the coconut aminos and apple cider vinegar. Season with the salt and mix well.

5. Reduce the heat to low and simmer for 5 to 8 minutes.

6. Turn off the heat and let the paste cool for a few minutes.

Approximate macros per serving: ————————
Calories: **113** • Fat: **10g** • Protein: **1g** • Net Carbs: **6g** • Fiber: **1g**

Ghee

YIELD: 2 cups, 1 tablespoon per serving • **PREP TIME:** 11 minutes
COOK TIME: 20 minutes

When I run out of ghee and I have some sticks of unsalted butter in the refrigerator, I like to make my own ghee. Using a nut milk bag is essential for filtering all the milk solids from that pot of liquid gold.

2 cups unsalted butter (4 sticks)

Special equipment:
Nut milk bag

1. Cut the sticks of butter into cubes and place them in a medium-sized saucepan.

2. Turn on the heat to medium-low. Let the butter melt slowly for about 10 minutes.

3. Using a spoon, carefully remove the white foam that rises to the top.

4. Continue to simmer the melted butter for 8 to 10 minutes, until the milk solids fall to the bottom and the liquid becomes clear.

5. Turn off the heat and let the liquid ghee cool for 10 minutes, so you won't burn yourself as you strain out the solids.

6. Place a fine-mesh nut milk bag inside a wide-mouth jar. Fold the top of the bag over the lip of the jar and secure the bag with a rubber band. Slowly pour the ghee into the jar. Carefully remove the nut milk bag and discard the milk solids left in it.

Let the ghee cool completely before covering. Store in the refrigerator for up to a month.

jenny's tip
If you have one available on hand, a good-quality mesh strainer will work as an alternative to a nut milk bag.

Approximate macros per serving: ─────────
Calories: **99** • Fat: **24g** • Protein: **0g** • Net Carbs: **0g** • Fiber: **0g**

Mayonnaise

 Cover the jar and store it in the refrigerator for up to a week.

YIELD: ¾ cup, 1 tablespoon per serving • **PREP TIME:** 3 minutes
COOK TIME: —

I usually buy ready-to-use mayonnaise for convenience, but when I unexpectedly run out and don't feel like running to the store, I make a fresh batch in less than 5 minutes. An immersion blender is great for this task, but a regular blender works if you don't have an immersion blender.

1 large egg, at room temperature

1 tablespoon freshly squeezed lemon juice (about ½ lemon)

½ teaspoon Dijon mustard

1 cup avocado oil, divided

¼ teaspoon sea salt

1. Place the egg, lemon juice, Dijon mustard, ¼ cup of the oil, and salt in a wide-mouth jar.

2. Use an immersion blender to blend the ingredients.

3. With the immersion blender still running, slowly drizzle the remaining ¾ cup of oil into the jar to emulsify the mayonnaise.

Approximate macros per serving: ———————
Calories: **171** • Fat: **19g** • Protein: **1g** • Net Carbs: **0g** • Fiber: **0g**

Build Your Plate

Blender Pancakes with Ghee, Oven-Baked Bacon, strawberries, blueberries

1. Place 4 Blender Pancakes (page 178) and 3 slices of bacon on each of two plates. Microwave each plate on high for 1 minute.

2. Place 1 tablespoon of ghee on top of each stack of the pancakes and add ¼ cup each of strawberries and blueberries to both plates.

Loaded Breakfast Frittata, Tomato Avocado Salad

1. Heat two servings of the Loaded Breakfast Frittata (page 180) in the microwave on high for 1 minute.

2. Transfer one serving of the frittata to each of two plates and add one serving of the Tomato Avocado Salad (page 202) to each plate.

Instant Pot Beef Barbacoa, Classic Veggie Fajitas, Tangy Onion and Jalapeño Relish, Aji Verde Sauce

1. Heat two servings of the Instant Pot Beef Barbacoa (page 186) and Classic Veggie Fajitas (page 196) in a skillet over medium-high heat for 2 minutes.

2. Divide between two plates and serve with ¼ cup of the Tangy Onion and Jalapeño Relish (page 204). Drizzle the barbacoa with 2 tablespoons of Aji Verde Sauce (page 206).

Black Pepper Chicken, Lo Mein

Plate two servings of the Black Pepper Chicken (page 190) and Lo Mein (page 194). Microwave on high for 1 to 2 minutes.

Five-Spice Meatballs, Shrimp Fried Rice, Chili Garlic Paste

1. Place one serving of the Five-Spice Meatballs (page 182) and Shrimp Fried Rice (page 192) on each of two plates. Microwave on high for 1 minute.

2. Place 1 tablespoon of the Chili Garlic Paste (page 208) on top of the warm meatballs to let it melt.

Chicken Korma, Garlic Naan

1. Place two servings of the Chicken Korma (page 184) in a bowl. Microwave on high for 1 minute.

2. Toast two servings (four slices) of the Garlic Naan (page 198) in a toaster oven at 350°F for 2 minutes or in a skillet over medium-high heat for 1 minute on each side.

3. Plate one serving of the Chicken Korma and the naan on each of two plates.

Easiest Lasagna

Plate two servings of the Easiest Lasagna. Microwave on high for 1 minute.

Part 3:
do it yourself

IMPLEMENTATION WEEK

Congratulations on successfully meal prepping these past four weeks! The work you've done with the done-for-you meal plans each week, even if you haven't prepped all the dishes, helps get you going to hone your meal prepping skills. Remember, it takes consistent practice to make meal prepping a habit and part of your keto lifestyle.

The week following week 4 of the done-for-you meal plans is what I call the Implementation Week. This is when you get creative and combine your favorite recipes from the first four weeks with the bonus recipes in this section to take a stab at building a customized weekly plan!

Building Your Own Weekly Plan

There is no right or wrong way to do things when it comes to meal prep. What matters is that you follow a method that works for you. If you want, you can go back to week 1 and follow it until week 4 again. However, creating your own meal plan is not as overwhelming as you may think because I've created a step-by-step Action Plan to help guide you. I've also provided two sample customized meal plans I created using some recipes from weeks 1 through 4 and the bonus recipes.

Incorporating Meal-Prepped Freezer Meals

Remember the recipes from each week that you froze for later? Now's the time to add them to your customized weekly plan so you can cut the number of recipes you cook each week in half! It's a good idea for each week's plan to include recipes that you can divide between eating that week and freezing for later so you'll always have something on hand to eat for future weeks.

The result is that you'll be doing less prepping and cooking because ready-to-eat meals will always be at your fingertips!

Action Plan

1. Print a blank meal plan calendar for the week and the recipe ideas worksheet from **easyketomealprep.com**.

2. On your recipe ideas worksheet, list your favorite recipes from weeks 1, 2, 3, and 4.

3. Go over the Bonus Recipes section on pages 221 through 245 and take note of the recipes you would like to make on your recipe ideas worksheet.

4. Pick two recipes for breakfast—one that makes four servings and another that makes six servings—and write them on your meal plan calendar for Monday to Friday.

5. Pick five main dishes and three or four sides to mix and match for lunch and dinner for Monday to Friday. If you have frozen meals available, you can choose from those as well.

6. Need snacks or treats? Pick one or two from the recipes on pages 247 through 301.

7. Once you've filled out your meal plan calendar, create your grocery list, and you're good to go!

Need more ideas?

Here are two customized meal plans that I've put together for you!

Customized Meal Plan #1

DAY	BREAKFAST	LUNCH	DINNER	SNACK
1	Instant Pot Eggs en Cocotte, Oven-Baked Bacon	Ginger Chicken, Ginger Scallion Sauce, Turmeric Garlic Cauliflower Rice	Sheet Pan Smoky Shrimp, Spaghetti Squash Noodles	Peanut Butter Cookies, Spiced Nut Mix, and Italian Cheese Roll-Ups
2	Instant Pot Eggs en Cocotte, Oven-Baked Bacon	Carne Asada (from the freezer), Zesty Slaw, Pico de Gallo	Kung Pao Chicken, Blanched Bok Choy	
3	Blender Pancakes, Ghee, Supercharged Nut Coffee	Sheet Pan Smoky Shrimp, Spaghetti Squash Noodles	Juicy Pan Fried Chicken Tenders, Nutty Tahini Broccoli	
4	Blender Pancakes, Ghee, Supercharged Nut Coffee	Carne Asada (from the freezer), Zesty Slaw, Pico de Gallo	Ginger Chicken, Ginger Scallion Sauce, Turmeric Garlic Cauliflower Rice	
5	Blender Pancakes, Ghee, Supercharged Nut Coffee	Kung Pao Chicken, Blanched Bok Choy	Juicy Pan-Fried Chicken Tenders, Nutty Tahini Broccoli	
6	Free Meal	Leftovers	Leftovers	
7	Free Meal	Leftovers	Leftovers	

Customized Meal Plan #2

DAY	BREAKFAST	LUNCH	DINNER	SNACK
1	Easy Peasy Hard-Boiled Eggs, Iced Matcha	Chicken Adobo, Turmeric Garlic Cauliflower Rice	Turkey Mushroom Sauté, Three-Veggie Chop Suey, Chili Oil	Nutty Chia Pudding, Peanut Butter Fat Bombs
2	Easy Peasy Hard-Boiled Eggs, Iced Matcha	Pesto Meatballs (from the freezer), Zucchini Noodles, Parmesan cheese	Instant Pot Roast, Jalapeño Cauliflower Mash	
3	Easy Peasy Hard-Boiled Eggs, Iced Matcha	Coconut Macadamia–Crusted Pork Chops, Basil Slaw	Turkey Mushroom Sauté, Three-Veggie Chop Suey, Chili Oil	
4	Italian Casserole, sliced avocados	Chicken Adobo, Turmeric Garlic Cauliflower Rice	Coconut Macadamia–Crusted Pork Chops, Basil Slaw	
5	Italian Casserole, sliced avocados	Instant Pot Roast, Jalapeño Cauliflower Mash	Pesto Meatballs (from the freezer), Zucchini Noodles, Parmesan cheese	
6	Free Meal	Leftovers	Leftovers	
7	Free Meal	Leftovers	Leftovers	

BONUS RECIPES

Instant Pot Eggs en Cocotte

SERVES 2 • **PREP TIME:** 3 minutes • **COOK TIME:** 5 minutes

Cover the dishes tightly with foil and store in the refrigerator for up to 3 days.

Remove the foil covering the ramekin. Microwave on high for 1 minute.

Jenny's tip
For firmer yolks, set the cook time to 6 to 7 minutes.

I only eat eggs three ways: poached, hard boiled using my Easy Peasy Hard-Boiled Eggs (page 52) technique, or baked. It usually took 10 to 15 minutes to make baked eggs in the oven, and I couldn't quite get the eggs cooked properly. More often than not, they turned out hard boiled! I've discovered that making these baked eggs in the Instant Pot takes no more than 5 minutes, and the eggs are perfectly soft-boiled every time.

2 teaspoons ghee, softened

4 large eggs

½ cup full-fat coconut milk

⅛ teaspoon sea salt

Pinch of black pepper

1 tablespoon chopped fresh chives, plus more for garnish

1 cup water

1. Coat the insides of two 4-ounce ramekins or cocotte dishes with the ghee.

2. Crack two eggs into each ramekin and pour the coconut milk on top. Season with the salt, pepper, and chives.

3. Pour the water into the Instant Pot and place a metal trivet at the bottom.

4. Place the two dishes on top of the trivet, cover the pot, and make sure the venting valve is set to the sealed position.

5. Press the Manual or Pressure Level button and cook on high pressure for 5 minutes.

6. Once the 5 minutes is up, cover the valve with a towel and flip the valve to release the pressure quickly. Remove the dishes immediately from the Instant Pot.

Approximate macros per serving:
Calories: **200** • Fat: **16g** • Protein: **13g** • Net Carbs: **1g** • Fiber: **0g**

Ginger Chicken

SERVES 4 · **PREP TIME:** 2 minutes · **COOK TIME:** 5 minutes

 Transfer the chicken to a glass container. Cover and store in the refrigerator for up to 5 days.

Reheat the chicken and the soup in the microwave separately, each for 1½ minutes.

This dish is inspired by the Hainanese Chicken (or simply Chinese Steamed Chicken) I grew up eating. It's typically a whole chicken cooked in boiling water and then served with rice, soup, and Ginger Scallion Sauce. Using chicken thighs instead of a whole chicken cuts down on the cooking time without sacrificing the flavor.

4 cups water

1 (1-inch) piece ginger, peeled and sliced

1 teaspoon sea salt

1 pound boneless, skinless chicken thighs

½ cup Ginger Scallion Sauce (page 240)

2 tablespoons sliced green onions

1. Pour the water into a medium-sized saucepan and add the ginger and salt. Bring to a boil over medium-high heat.

2. Place the chicken in the water and poach for 5 minutes. Remove the chicken and slice it into 1-inch pieces. Then slather it with half of the Ginger Scallion Sauce. Save the other half of the sauce to serve on the side.

3. Strain the broth to remove any excess protein bits that may cloud the soup. Top with the green onions and serve with the chicken.

Approximate macros per serving:
Calories: **275** · Fat: **19g** · Protein: **23g** · Net Carbs: **4g** · Fiber: **1g**

Kung Pao Chicken

SERVES 4 • **PREP TIME:** 5 minutes, plus 15 minutes to marinate
COOK TIME: 7 minutes

This Kung Pao Chicken recipe has no added sugars or sweeteners because the coconut aminos already adds the right amount of sweetness! I highly recommend using my Chili Garlic Paste as the aromatic for this dish because it seriously provides the best flavor, and it cuts down your prep time because you have it ready to use in your refrigerator!

Transfer the chicken to a glass container. Cover and store in the refrigerator for up to 5 days.

Reheat the chicken in the microwave on high for 2 minutes.

Jenny's tip

Want to kick up the spice level even more? Add another tablespoon of chili oil on top.

1 pound boneless, skinless chicken thighs, cut into 1-inch pieces

¼ cup coconut aminos, divided

1 tablespoon unseasoned rice vinegar

1 tablespoon avocado oil

1 tablespoon Chili Garlic Paste (page 208)

1 medium zucchini, diced

1 red bell pepper, diced

1 tablespoon Chili Oil (page 116)

1½ teaspoons sea salt

1 teaspoon black pepper

¼ cup roasted peanuts

1. Place the chicken, 2 tablespoons of the coconut aminos, and the rice vinegar in a small bowl. Mix and cover with foil, then place it in the refrigerator to marinate for 15 minutes.

2. Heat a wok or large skillet over medium-high heat. Once it begins to smoke, pour in the avocado oil and swirl to coat the bottom evenly.

3. Place the chicken in the pan and sauté for 2 minutes. Season with the Chili Garlic Paste; sauté and cook for 2 minutes.

4. Add the zucchini and bell pepper; sauté for another 2 minutes.

5. Season the Kung Pao Chicken with the remaining 1 tablespoon of the coconut aminos, chili oil, salt, and pepper. Add the peanuts and mix well. Cook for one more minute, then remove from the heat.

Approximate macros per serving:
Calories: **261** • Fat: **14g** • Protein: **23g** • Net Carbs: **8g** • Fiber: **1g**

Coconut Macadamia–Crusted Pork Chops

SERVES 4 • **PREP TIME:** 8 minutes • **COOK TIME:** 10 minutes

The combination of coconut and macadamia always reminds me of the warm breeze and sunny skies in Hawaii. If you're tired of your regular pan-fried seasoned pork chops, you've gotta make this coconut macadamia–crusted version.

¼ cup crushed macadamia nuts

¼ cup unsweetened shredded coconut

4 thin-cut boneless pork chops (1 pound)

Olive oil spray

¾ teaspoon sea salt

½ teaspoon black pepper

1. Preheat the oven to 375°F.

2. Combine the macadamia nuts and shredded coconut in a small bowl.

3. Layer a couple of paper towels on a plate and place the pork chops side by side on top of the towels. Using another piece of paper towel, pat the tops of each pork chop to remove any excess liquid from the chops.

4. Lightly coat a rimmed baking sheet with the olive oil spray.

5. Season both sides of the pork chops with the salt and pepper. Place the pork chops on the baking sheet in one layer and spoon the macadamia nut and coconut mixture on top of each chop. Bake for 10 minutes.

Transfer the pork chops to a glass container. Cover and store in the refrigerator for up to 5 days.

Reheat the pork chops in the toaster oven on the toast or high setting for 2 minutes.

jenny's tips

If using thick-cut pork chops, increase the cooking time by 5 minutes.

Use a food processor or a good ol' mortar and pestle to crush the macadamia nuts into small pieces.

Approximate macros per serving:
Calories: **332** • Fat: **23g** • Protein: **28g** • Net Carbs: **0g** • Fiber: **1g**

Juicy Pan-Fried Chicken Tenders

Transfer the chicken to a glass container. Cover and store in the refrigerator for up to 5 days.

Heat the chicken in the microwave on high for 1 minute or on a skillet over medium-high heat for 1 minute each side.

SERVES 4 • **PREP TIME:** 2 minutes • **COOK TIME:** 6 minutes

One of the easiest recipes I've made uses chicken tenders, a generous serving of spices, and a hot oiled pan. Covering the chicken for a short time as it cooks ensures that the tenders turn out juicy. No one wants tough and dried-out chicken!

1 pound chicken tenders

1½ tablespoons 10-Spice Seasoning (page 244) or any seasoning of your choice

2 tablespoons avocado oil

1. Coat the chicken tenders on both sides with the 10-Spice Seasoning.

2. Heat the avocado oil in a large cast-iron pan or skillet over medium-high heat. Swirl the oil to coat the bottom of the pan.

3. Place the chicken tenders on the pan in one layer, making sure they don't overlap. Cover and cook for 3 minutes. Flip and cook for another 3 minutes.

4. The chicken is done once the juices run clear when you pierce the tenders with a fork. Remove from the heat immediately to prevent the chicken from overcooking.

Approximate macros per serving:
Calories: **186** • Fat: **8g** • Protein: **23g** • Net Carbs: **4g** • Fiber: **1g**

Asian Glazed Halibut

SERVES 4 · **PREP TIME:** 5 minutes · **COOK TIME:** 7 minutes

Transfer the fish and sauce to a glass container. Cover and store in the refrigerator for up to 3 days.

Heat the fish and sauce in the microwave on high for 1 minute.

Mild, flaky white fish such as halibut tastes great with a zesty Asian glaze made with lime juice, garlic, and ginger. If you can't find halibut, substitute any white fish of your choice.

Juice of 2 limes (about ¼ cup)

¼ cup coconut aminos

1 (1½-inch) piece ginger, peeled and grated (about ¾ tablespoon)

3 cloves garlic, minced

1 pound halibut fillets

½ teaspoon sea salt

½ teaspoon black pepper

1 tablespoon avocado oil

1. Prepare the sauce by mixing the lime juice, coconut aminos, ginger, and garlic in a small bowl.

2. Pat the halibut fillets dry with paper towels and season both sides with the salt and pepper.

3. Heat a large cast-iron pan over high heat. Once it begins to smoke, pour in the avocado oil and place the halibut fillets in the pan.

4. Sear the first side for 1 minute. Flip and sear the other side for 1 minute.

5. Reduce the heat to medium-low and slowly pour the sauce over the fish. Let simmer for 5 minutes, until the sauce has thickened.

Approximate macros per serving:
Calories: **171** · Fat: **6g** · Protein: **22g** · Net Carbs: **6g** · Fiber: **0g**

Sheet Pan Smoky Shrimp

Transfer the shrimp to a glass container. Cover and store in the refrigerator for up to 3 days.

Heat the shrimp in the microwave on high for 1 minute.

SERVES 4 • **PREP TIME:** 3 minutes • **COOK TIME:** 10 minutes

Shrimp cooks so fast that it's my protein of choice when I'm short on time and need to have a meal ready ASAP. Here I toss it with some taco seasoning and sweet red bell peppers and pop it in the oven—that's it!

1 pound large raw shrimp, peeled and deveined

1 red bell pepper, sliced

1 teaspoon olive oil

1½ teaspoons taco seasoning

Juice of 2 limes (about ¼ cup)

½ cup chopped fresh cilantro

1. Preheat the oven to 400°F.

2. Place the shrimp and bell pepper slices in a large bowl. Drizzle the olive oil on top and season with the taco seasoning. Toss to coat the shrimp and peppers evenly.

3. Arrange the shrimp and peppers in one layer on a rimmed baking sheet. Bake for 10 minutes. The shrimp is done once it's pink and has curled up. Season with the lime juice and top with the cilantro.

Approximate macros per serving:
Calories: **153** • Fat: **3g** • Protein: **24g** • Net Carbs: **5g** • Fiber: **2g**

Instant Pot Salsa Chicken

SERVES 8 • **PREP TIME:** 1 minute, plus 5 minutes to cool
COOK TIME: 15 minutes, plus 25 minutes to release pressure

No recipe is easier than this Instant Pot Salsa Chicken. It has just six ingredients, and the prep time is less than one minute, so it's one of my go-to recipes that never fails. The chicken shreds easily with two forks once it's done!

 Cover the glass container and store in the refrigerator for up to 5 days.

Heat the chicken with the salsa in the microwave on high for 2 minutes.

2 pounds boneless, skinless chicken thighs

½ teaspoon sea salt

½ teaspoon ground cumin

1 (24-ounce) jar red salsa, divided

Juice of 1 lime (about 2 tablespoons)

½ cup chopped fresh cilantro

1. Season the chicken with the salt and cumin and then place it in the Instant Pot. Pour in half of the salsa.

2. Seal the lid and make sure the vent is set to the sealing position. Press the Manual or Pressure Level button and cook on high pressure for 15 minutes.

3. Once the timer beeps, allow the pressure to release naturally for 25 minutes. The chicken will cook a little more during this time.

4. Remove the lid and let the chicken cool for 5 minutes, until it's no longer steaming. Use two forks to shred the chicken in the Instant Pot. Transfer the chicken to a glass container, excluding the excess liquid that was produced. Pour the remaining half of the salsa on top of the chicken and mix.

Approximate macros per serving:
Calories: **178** • Fat: **6g** • Protein: **24g** • Net Carbs: **1g** • Fiber: **6g**

Basil Slaw

SERVES 4 • **PREP TIME:** 5 minutes, plus 23 minutes to chill
COOK TIME: 1 minute

If you're eating the slaw on another day, transfer it to a glass container and store in the refrigerator for up to 2 days.

Mixing fresh herbs such as basil into regular coleslaw adds a nice hint of sweetness. The slaw comes together quickly, so you'll have a light and refreshing side dish in no time. Try it with the Everything Baked Chicken (page 62), Instant Pot Roast (page 146), or Coconut Macadamia–Crusted Pork Chops (page 228).

1 pound bagged coleslaw mix

3 tablespoons fresh basil, chopped

2 tablespoons Mayonnaise (page 212)

¼ teaspoon black pepper

1. Fill a medium-sized saucepan halfway with water and bring to a boil.

2. Place the coleslaw mix in the water and blanch for 30 seconds to soften it slightly.

3. Drain immediately and let it cool for 8 minutes.

4. Transfer the cooled coleslaw to a medium-sized bowl and add the fresh basil and mayonnaise; season with the pepper. Mix well, cover, and refrigerate for 15 minutes to chill.

Approximate macros per serving:
Calories: **72** • Fat: **5g** • Protein: **1g** • Net Carbs: **4g** • Fiber: **3g**

Ginger Scallion Sauce

Let the Ginger Scallion Sauce cool for 10 minutes, then transfer it to a pint-sized mason jar. Cover and store in the refrigerator for up to a week.

jenny's tips

If you're having a hard time grating fresh ginger, throw it in the freezer the day before. Frozen ginger is much easier to grate!

This sauce is best served cold with reheated chicken.

SERVES ½ cup, 1 tablespoon per serving • **PREP TIME:** 10 minutes
COOK TIME: 5 minutes

Like my Chili Oil (page 116) and Chili Garlic Paste (page 208), this Ginger Scallion Sauce is a condiment that you can add to almost anything. Top hard-boiled eggs with it, mix it with cooked cauliflower rice, or use it with grilled meat or Ginger Chicken (page 224). This has been one of my flavor-booster staples for the past five years, and I never get tired of it!

1 cup chopped green onions (green and white parts)

1 (4-inch) piece ginger, peeled and grated (about 2 tablespoons)

1 teaspoon unseasoned rice vinegar or apple cider vinegar

½ teaspoon sea salt

¼ cup avocado oil

1. Place the green onions, ginger, vinegar, and salt in a medium heatproof dish.

2. Pour the avocado oil in a small saucepan and warm over medium heat for 5 minutes. The oil is ready once it begins to smoke.

3. Turn off the heat. Carefully pour the hot oil into the heatproof dish with the green onion and ginger mixture. It will sizzle immediately upon contact.

4. Mix everything together until the green onions and ginger are soft.

Approximate macros per serving: ————————
Calories: **71** • Fat: **7g** • Protein: **0g** • Net Carbs: **2g** • Fiber: **0g**

Giardiniera

 Store in the refrigerator for up to 2 weeks.

SERVES 4 • **PREP TIME:** 10 minutes, plus 3 days to marinate
COOK TIME: —

Giardiniera always reminds me of Italian delis that serve salads and sandwiches with tangy pickled vegetables. I combined three low-carb vegetables with some herbs and seasonings to make giardiniera right at home. Brining the vegetables overnight helps preserve and prepare them for pickling the next day.

2 cups cauliflower florets, cut into small pieces

2 cups green beans, cut in half

1 red bell pepper, sliced

4 cloves garlic, sliced

6 cups water

2 teaspoons sea salt

½ cup olive oil

½ cup red wine vinegar

2 teaspoons ground dried oregano

1 teaspoon black pepper

1. Place the cauliflower, green beans, bell pepper, and garlic in a gallon-sized zip-top bag. Pour in the water and season with the sea salt. Press to remove the excess air, seal the bag, and refrigerate to brine overnight.

2. Empty the zip-top bag into a colander to drain the brine from the vegetables.

3. Transfer the vegetables to two wide-mouth quart-sized mason jars.

4. In a small bowl, whisk together the olive oil, vinegar, oregano, and pepper. Evenly divide the oil mixture between the two jars. Cover and store in the refrigerator for 3 days before eating.

Approximate macros per serving: —
Calories: **299** • Fat: **27g** • Protein: **3g** • Net Carbs: **6g** • Fiber: **4g**

10-Spice Seasoning

SERVES 1½ tablespoons, 1½ tablespoons per serving
PREP TIME: 3 minutes • **COOK TIME:** —

I used Trader Joe's 21 Seasoning Salute for the longest time, but I finally came up with a blend that tastes even better and has fewer ingredients!

1 teaspoon garlic powder

1 teaspoon onion powder

½ teaspoon sea salt

½ teaspoon black pepper

¼ teaspoon dried thyme

¼ teaspoon ground dried oregano

¼ teaspoon dried rosemary

⅛ teaspoon dried basil

⅛ teaspoon ground cumin

Pinch of cayenne pepper

Combine all the ingredients in a small bowl and mix well. Transfer to a small glass container, cover tightly, and store in the pantry at room temperature for future use.

Approximate macros per serving:
Calories: **24** • Fat: **0g** • Protein: **1g** • Net Carbs: **4g** • Fiber: **1g**

SNACKS, TREATS, AND DRINK RECIPES

Seed Crackers

Place the crackers in a glass container and store at room temperature for up to a week.

SERVES 10 crackers, 2 crackers per serving · **PREP TIME:** 2 minutes, plus 45 minutes for resting and cooling time · **COOK TIME:** 30 minutes

There are commercial brands of seed crackers that are widely available now, but homemade is still cheaper and tastes better. I made some seed crackers years ago when I started eating gluten-free, and I remember really enjoying them. Here's my updated version with a few tweaks to make it keto-friendly.

½ cup water

½ cup flax seeds, whole

¼ cup raw pepitas

¼ cup hulled raw sunflower seeds

2 tablespoons sesame seeds

½ teaspoon sea salt

½ teaspoon black pepper

1. Combine all the ingredients in a medium-sized bowl and let sit at room temperature for 30 minutes. Stir every 10 minutes to check whether the mixture has thickened and the seeds are absorbing the water.

2. Preheat the oven to 250°F.

3. Line a rimmed baking sheet with parchment paper.

4. Use a tablespoon to scoop the seed mixture onto the prepared baking sheet and use the back of the spoon to flatten each scoop until it's thin and about 3 inches in diameter. The thinner the better, so the crackers will be crispy.

5. Bake the first side for 20 minutes. Carefully flip each cracker with a silicone turner and bake for 10 more minutes. Remove from the oven and let cool on the baking sheet for 15 minutes. You'll know they're done when they're crispy and no longer wet and soft.

Approximate macros per serving:
Calories: **145** · Fat: **11g** · Protein: **8g** · Net Carbs: **1g** · Fiber: **5g**

Parmesan Crisps Three Ways

 Let the crisps cool completely, then transfer to a zip-top bag and store at room temperature for up to a week.

SERVES 16 crisps, 2 crisps per serving • **PREP TIME:** 5 minutes
COOK TIME: 24 minutes

When I first started eating keto, I was always on the hunt for a crunchy and salty snack because my beloved carb-filled nacho chips were out. I defaulted to munching on pork rinds. After a while, though, I got tired of them and wanted something else. Enter these wafer-thin Parmesan crisps! You can buy them at the grocery store, but, of course, it's always much better and cheaper to make them at home. Enjoy them plain, or add a few mix-ins to make smoky chipotle or black pepper rosemary–flavored crisps!

1½ cups shredded Parmesan cheese

¼ teaspoon chipotle powder

¼ teaspoon dried rosemary, roughly chopped

⅛ teaspoon black pepper

1. Preheat the oven to 375°F. Line a rimmed baking sheet with parchment paper.

2. Divide the Parmesan cheese evenly into three small bowls.

3. Season one bowl with the chipotle powder and another with the rosemary and black pepper. Stir each one to combine. Leave the third bowl plain.

4. Cook one flavor at a time, starting with the plain Parmesan cheese.

5. Scoop heaping tablespoons of the plain Parmesan onto the baking sheet, spacing them 1 inch apart, so there's enough room for the crisps to spread while they cook.

6. Bake for 8 minutes. Remove from the baking sheet immediately and transfer to a baking rack to cool.

7. Wipe the parchment with a paper towel to remove the excess oil and any leftover cheese bits. Prepare the chipotle crisps, then the rosemary and black pepper, baking each batch for 8 minutes.

Approximate macros per serving:
Calories: **312** • Fat: **21g** • Protein: **28g** • Net Carbs: **3g** • Fiber: **0g**

Pepperoni Pizza Bites

SERVES 2 • **PREP TIME:** 2 minutes, plus 3 minutes to cool
COOK TIME: 10 minutes

One time I was craving pizza, but all we had in the refrigerator was cheese and pepperoni, so I decided to bake them together for a fun snack. At first Will thought it was pretty odd, but he ended up enjoying them as well.

1 ounce sliced pepperoni

½ cup shredded goat's milk or sheep's milk cheddar or mozzarella cheese

½ teaspoon red pepper flakes (optional)

1. Preheat the oven to 375°F. Line a rimmed baking sheet with parchment paper.

2. Arrange the pepperoni in a single layer on the lined baking sheet without overlapping the slices. Evenly distribute the cheese on top of the pepperoni. Sprinkle with the red pepper flakes for an extra kick.

3. Bake for 10 minutes, until the cheese is melted and bubbly. Let cool for 3 minutes before eating so you don't burn your mouth.

Approximate macros per serving:
Calories: **42** • Fat: **8g** • Protein: **2g** • Net Carbs: **0g** • Fiber: **0g**

Packable Cheese Board

SERVES 4 • **PREP TIME:** 10 minutes • **COOK TIME:** —

I have mad love for cheese boards. What could be better than meat and cheese together? Gone are the days of trying to figure out what to bring to potlucks and parties. Now I always bring a cheese board with a variety of goodies on it. Making this keto version is not that hard because you easily can substitute Seed Crackers and Parmesan Crisps for regular crackers.

1 ounce fresh goat cheese, softened

¼ cup olive oil

4 ounces pepperoni

2 ounces goat's milk or cow's milk cheddar cheese, cubed

¾ cup olives (Castelvetrano or Kalamata or a mix of both)

½ cup Spiced Nut Mix (page 262)

½ batch Seed Crackers (page 248)

½ batch Parmesan Crisps Three Ways (page 250)

1. Place the goat cheese in a small bowl and pour the olive oil on top. Position the bowl in the corner of a wooden board or large serving platter.

2. Arrange the pepperoni and cheddar evenly on the board.

3. Place the olives and Spiced Nut Mix in separate small bowls and insert them between the pepperoni and cheddar.

4. Carefully place the Seed Crackers and Parmesan Crisps under the pepperoni and cheddar to secure them on the board. Voilà! Wasn't that easy?

Approximate macros per serving:
Calories: **578** • Fat: **52g** • Protein: **30g** • Net Carbs: **4g** • Fiber: **4g**

Crudité Platter with Herbed Dip

SERVES 4 • **PREP TIME:** 10 minutes, plus 30 minutes chilling time
COOK TIME: 1 minute

Like the Packable Cheese Board (page 254), this crudité platter is a great crowd-pleasing and party-friendly snack to bring to a gathering. It features an array of bright and colorful vegetables served with a rich, creamy dip. Don't skip the blanching step, which makes the tougher veggies, such as broccolini, easier to eat. The quick hot water bath also brightens the color to make the veggies pop!

jenny's tips

Soften the cream cheese in the microwave for 15 seconds.

If you don't have an immersion blender, a regular blender will work. You also can whisk the dip with a wire whisk.

If you can't find purple cauliflower, any color will work.

FOR THE HERBED DIP:

4 ounces cream cheese (½ cup), softened

¼ cup plus 2 tablespoons full-fat coconut milk

1 large clove garlic, minced (about 1 teaspoon)

¼ teaspoon sea salt

¼ cup finely chopped fresh chives

FOR THE CRUDITÉ PLATTER:

4 ounces broccolini, bottom stems removed

4 ounces purple cauliflower florets

4 ounces sugar snap peas

2 ounces cherry tomatoes

1. Place all the dip ingredients except the chives in a mug. Using an immersion blender, puree the dip to make it smooth and creamy. Stir in the chives, cover, and refrigerate for 30 minutes to allow the flavors to blend.

2. While the dip is in the refrigerator, fill a large saucepan with water and bring to a boil.

3. Prepare an ice bath by filling a large bowl with cold water and a couple of cups of ice.

4. Blanch the broccolini for 30 seconds. Immediately transfer it to the ice bath to chill. Next, blanch the cauliflower florets for 30 seconds. Immediately transfer them to the ice bath with the broccolini.

5. Drain the veggies in a colander and pat them dry with paper towels.

6. Fill a rimmed baking pan with ice to use as a serving platter. Arrange the broccolini, cauliflower, sugar snap peas, and cherry tomatoes on top. Serve the dip on the side.

Approximate macros per serving: ———
Calories: **219** • Fat: **13g** • Protein: **14g** • Net Carbs: **10g** • Fiber: **10g**

Deviled Eggs

SERVES 12 deviled eggs, 3 eggs per serving • **PREP TIME:** 10 minutes
COOK TIME: —

I've tasted different varieties of deviled eggs—from simple to fancy—and I will always pick this classic version that has the right amount of mayonnaise and mustard so you can still taste the richness of the egg in that one delectable bite.

6 Easy Peasy Hard-Boiled Eggs (page 52)

½ cup Mayonnaise (page 212)

1 tablespoon Dijon mustard

½ teaspoon paprika

2 tablespoons chopped fresh chives

1. Cut the hard-boiled eggs diagonally in half and scoop the yolks into a medium-sized bowl. Arrange the whites cut side up on a serving platter.

2. Mix the mayonnaise, mustard, and paprika with the yolks and stir until smooth and creamy.

3. Transfer the egg yolk mixture to a zip-top sandwich bag and press gently to remove as much air as possible before sealing. Snip off one corner of the bag and pipe the filling into the egg whites. Top each one with chives.

jenny's tip

Looking for fun, colorful eggs? Try swapping the mayonnaise for mashed avocados!

Approximate macros per serving:
Calories: **328** • Fat: **30g** • Protein: **13g** • Net Carbs: **1g** • Fiber: **0g**

Guacamole and Pork Rinds

SERVES 4 • **PREP TIME:** 5 minutes • **COOK TIME:** —

I can eat an entire bag of pork rinds and a bowl of this guacamole without shame! A little bit of chopped jalapeño pepper gives the guac some heat without being overpowering.

FOR THE GUACAMOLE:

2 Hass avocados, peeled and pitted

1 shallot, finely chopped

1 jalapeño pepper, seeded and finely chopped

Juice of 1 lime (about 2 tablespoons)

1 teaspoon garlic powder

½ teaspoon sea salt

1 (2-ounce) bag pork rinds, for serving

In a medium-sized bowl, combine all the guacamole ingredients. Use a fork to mash the avocados and mix everything together. Enjoy with some pork rinds on the side.

Approximate macros per serving:
Calories: **51** • Fat: **3g** • Protein: **1g** • Net Carbs: **5g** • Fiber: **3g**

Spiced Nut Mix

SERVES 8 • **PREP TIME:** 2 minutes • **COOK TIME:** 25 minutes

Let the nut mix cool completely, then transfer to a mason jar. Cover tightly and store at room temperature for up to a week.

Will and I were snacking on a fresh batch of this nut mix, and it was hard to stop after just a handful! This sweet, savory, salty, and buttery goodness is a great party appetizer and a fun addition to a charcuterie board.

¼ cup raw cashews

¼ cup raw pecan halves

¼ cup raw pepitas

¼ teaspoon garlic powder

¼ teaspoon paprika

⅛ teaspoon sea salt

⅛ teaspoon black pepper

½ teaspoon ghee

1. Preheat the oven to 300°F.

2. Spread the nuts and pepitas evenly on a rimmed baking sheet.

3. Roast for 25 minutes, stirring halfway through cooking to make sure the nuts and seeds cook evenly.

4. While the nuts and seeds are roasting, combine the garlic powder, paprika, salt, and pepper in a small bowl and set aside.

5. Transfer the roasted nuts and seeds to a medium-sized bowl and toss with the ghee.

6. Sprinkle the seasoning all over the ghee-covered nut mixture. Toss to coat evenly with the spices.

Approximate macros per serving:
Calories: **74** • Fat: **7g** • Protein: **2g** • Net Carbs: **2g** • Fiber: **1g**

Instant Pot Chicken Wings

SERVES 4 · **PREP TIME:** 5 minutes · **COOK TIME:** 25 minutes

Transfer the wings to a glass container. Cover and refrigerate for up to 5 days.

Are you a wing lover? Look no further, because these flavor-packed Instant Pot Chicken Wings will be your new favorite! This Instant Pot method cuts cooking time in half. A 6-quart pot can hold a lot of wings, so it's easy to make a big batch that's enough for up to four people.

FOR THE DRY RUB:

1½ tablespoons onion powder

2 teaspoons chili powder

2 teaspoons black pepper

2 teaspoons sea salt

1 teaspoon paprika

3 pounds chicken wings

1 cup water

1. Combine all the ingredients for the dry rub in a small bowl and mix together.

2. Place the chicken wings in a large bowl and season with the dry rub. Toss the chicken until each wing is evenly seasoned.

3. Pour the water into the Instant Pot and place a metal rack at the bottom. Stack the wings evenly on the metal rack.

4. Seal the lid and make sure the valve is set to the sealed position.

5. Press the Manual or Pressure Level button and cook for 15 minutes on high pressure.

6. Once the wings are done cooking, cover the valve with a towel and flip the valve to release the pressure quickly.

7. Preheat the oven broiler to high.

8. Set a baking rack on top of a rimmed baking sheet.

9. Arrange the chicken wings side by side on top of the rack. Make sure the wings are in one layer and do not overlap.

10. Broil for 5 minutes. Flip the wings and broil for another 5 minutes.

Approximate macros per serving:
Calories: **473** · Fat: **30g** · Protein: **38g** · Net Carbs: **10g** · Fiber: **0g**

Garlic Parmesan Chicken Wings

SERVES 4 • **PREP TIME:** 15 minutes • **COOK TIME:** 35 minutes

Transfer the wings to a glass container. Cover and refrigerate for up to 5 days.

These Garlic Parmesan Chicken Wings are inspired by this joint near my place called Wing Stop. Whenever my mom and my brother, Carlo, would come over, we would walk over to Wing Stop and order a bunch of tasty wings. My mom loves the garlic Parmesan wings, and I've always wanted to re-create that recipe, so I finally did! Baking these in the oven on a baking rack helps the wings cook evenly on both sides so the skin crisps up nicely without using a ton of oil. The rack also helps excess fat drain away from the wings so they don't become soggy as they cook.

2 pounds chicken wings

1½ teaspoons sea salt

2 tablespoons ghee

4 cloves garlic, minced (about 4 teaspoons)

¼ cup shredded or grated Parmesan cheese

½ teaspoon black pepper

1 teaspoon red pepper flakes (optional)

1. Preheat the oven to 400°F.

2. Line a rimmed baking sheet with foil and set a baking rack on top.

3. Pat the chicken wings dry to remove as much moisture as possible. Season both sides with the salt.

4. Place the wings on the rack, making sure they're evenly spaced.

5. Bake for 15 minutes. Flip and bake for another 15 minutes.

6. Turn the oven to broil and broil for 5 more minutes, until the skin turns golden brown. Make sure to watch the wings closely so they don't burn!

7. While the chicken is cooking, heat a small pan over medium heat.

8. Sauté the ghee and garlic for 1 minute, until the garlic is fragrant. Set aside to cool.

9. In a small bowl, mix the cheese, black pepper, and red pepper flakes.

10. Place the cooked chicken wings in a large bowl and pour the garlic ghee all over them. Use two spoons to toss the wings to coat them with the ghee.

11. Sprinkle the cheese mixture on top and toss the wings some more to combine.

Approximate macros per serving: ———————
Calories: **578** • Fat: **38g** • Protein: **47g** • Net Carbs: **10g** • Fiber: **0g**

Italian Roll-Ups

SERVES 2 · **PREP TIME:** 10 minutes · **COOK TIME:** —

I crushed a few rolls one time when I was snacking on these! Goat cheese and basil elevate deli meat a notch. Prepare these no-cook snacks in the evening and pack them to enjoy on the go the next day.

Transfer to a glass container and store in the refrigerator for up to 2 days.

4 ounces prosciutto

4 ounces mortadella or ham

2 ounces fresh goat cheese

1 bunch fresh basil leaves

1. Layer pieces of prosciutto and mortadella on top of each other on a chopping board. Place a couple of the basil leaves on the mortadella, then add a scoop of the goat cheese to cover the basil.

2. Roll tightly, starting from one corner to the other. Slice diagonally in half.

Approximate macros per serving: Calories: **378** · Fat: **26g** · Protein: **34g** · Net Carbs: **1g** · Fiber: **0g**

Pork Rind Nachos

SERVES 2 • **PREP TIME:** 10 minutes • **COOK TIME:** 5 minutes

Say what?! Pork rinds instead of chips in nachos? Heck yeah! This ultimate keto-friendly snack will easily become one of your favorites. Put together a tray to share or enjoy on your own. Light and crunchy clouds of pork goodness with a heap of Instant Pot Roast plus all the fixin's will satisfy your snack cravings.

1 (2-ounce) bag pork rinds

1 cup shredded Instant Pot Roast (page 146)

½ cup sliced black olives

½ cup Pico de Gallo (page 118)

½ cup shredded cheddar or mozzarella cheese or fresh goat cheese

2 tablespoons chopped fresh cilantro

1. Preheat the oven broiler to low.

2. Place the pork rinds in one layer on a baking sheet. Spread the roast and olives on top.

3. Drain any excess liquid from the pico de gallo and evenly distribute half on top of the beef. Sprinkle the cheese over the top and broil for 5 minutes, until the cheese is melted.

4. Top with the remaining pico de gallo and cilantro and serve.

jenny's tip

It's important to drain the excess liquid from the pico de gallo to help prevent the pork rinds from getting soggy, although some may soften during broiling no matter what. If desired, add all the pico de gallo immediately before eating instead of dividing it.

Approximate macros per serving:
Calories: **392** • Fat: **19g** • Protein: **37g** • Net Carbs: **8g** • Fiber: **4g**

Peanut Butter Cookies

SERVES 12, 1 cookie per serving • **PREP TIME:** 5 minutes, plus 10 minutes cooling time • **COOK TIME:** 10 minutes

Three-ingredient cookies? Yes, please! If you're like me and aren't much of a baker, these foolproof peanut butter cookies will be right up your alley. Also, you won't be able to tell there's no flour in them. Winner? I think so!

1 cup unsweetened peanut butter

1 large egg

½ cup granulated Swerve

1. Preheat the oven to 350°F. Line a rimmed baking sheet with parchment paper.

2. Place all the ingredients in a large bowl and mix well until a dough forms.

3. Fill a small cookie scoop or a teaspoon with the dough and press it on the parchment-lined baking sheet. Make sure to leave 1 inch of space between the cookies.

4. Slightly flatten the tops of the cookies by pressing with a fork vertically then horizontally to create a crosshatch pattern.

5. Bake for 10 minutes. Once the cookies are done, immediately remove them from the oven; let them cool and firm up on the pan for 10 minutes. Don't try to remove the cookies from the pan while they're hot because they will crumble!

6. After the cookies have firmed up, transfer them to a baking rack to cool completely.

Place the cookies in an airtight container or zip-top bag and store at room temperature for up to 3 days.

jenny's tip

Want the cookies to taste more peanut buttery? Reduce the Swerve from ½ cup to ¼ cup.

Approximate macros per serving: ─────────
Calories: **209** • Fat: **18g** • Protein: **8g** • Net Carbs: **4g** • Fiber: **3g**

Nutty Chia Pudding

SERVES 2 • **PREP TIME:** 10 minutes, plus time to chill overnight
COOK TIME: 6 minutes

I'd never really jumped on the chia pudding bandwagon. But that recently changed when I started mixing in toasted shredded coconut and sliced almonds, which add a nice crunch and texture. Coconut butter makes the pudding taste like a decadent treat!

¼ cup unsweetened shredded coconut

¼ cup sliced almonds

½ cup full-fat coconut milk

¼ cup chia seeds

¼ cup water

2 tablespoons coconut butter, softened

20 drops liquid stevia

1. Heat a large cast-iron pan over low heat.

2. Place the shredded coconut in the pan and stir for 1 minute, until lightly toasted. This will happen fast, so keep an eye on it. Transfer the toasted coconut to a pint-sized mason jar and set aside.

3. In the same pan still over low heat, toast the almonds for 5 minutes, until lightly browned. Stir occasionally to prevent burning. Transfer the toasted almonds to the same jar as the shredded coconut. Stir to combine and let cool for a few minutes before covering tightly.

4. Combine the coconut milk, chia seeds, water, coconut butter, and stevia in a medium-sized bowl. Stir to combine and let sit for 1 minute. Stir some more to prevent the chia seeds from clumping together in big chunks. Let sit again for 1 minute. Stir and let sit a couple more times until the mixture has a yogurtlike texture.

5. Divide the chia pudding evenly between two pint-sized mason jars or dessert cups. Cover and refrigerate overnight.

6. Just before serving, top the pudding with the toasted coconut and almonds for some nutty and crunchy goodness with each spoonful.

Store any extra pudding in the refrigerator for up to 2 days.

jenny's tips

Swap the almonds for your favorite nuts or seeds. Pecans or pepitas are a great choice.

To quickly soften coconut butter, place it in a small microwave-safe bowl and microwave on high.

Approximate macros per serving:
Calories: **368** • Fat: **29g** • Protein: **12g** • Net Carbs: **3g** • Fiber: **14g**

Chocolate Bark

Transfer to a zip-top bag and store in the refrigerator for up to a week.

jenny's tip

Ceremonial matcha is a little pricier than culinary matcha, but it has a bright green color and a mild taste. If you don't want to spring for the ceremonial kind, the more affordable culinary matcha works as well.

SERVES 8 • **PREP TIME:** 10 minutes, plus 55 minutes cooling time
COOK TIME: 6 minutes

This chocolate bark is a feast for the eyes and palate thanks to the contrast of the bright green matcha against the dark chocolate. Keep a batch in the refrigerator for a ready-to-eat keto treat!

¼ cup unsweetened shredded coconut

¼ cup sliced almonds

1 teaspoon matcha powder

8 ounces 90% dark chocolate

2 tablespoons cacao butter

20 drops liquid stevia

1. Heat a large cast-iron pan or skillet over low heat.

2. Place the coconut in the pan and stir for 1 minute until lightly toasted. This will happen fast, so keep an eye on it. Transfer to a small bowl and set aside.

3. Toast the sliced almonds in the same pan for 5 minutes, until lightly browned. Stir occasionally to prevent burning. Transfer the toasted almonds to the bowl with the shredded coconut.

4. Sprinkle the matcha powder on the almonds and coconut and stir to mix well. Set aside while you prepare the chocolate.

5. Pour water into a small saucepan until the pan is one-quarter full and bring to a boil over medium-high heat.

6. Turn off the heat and place a heatproof bowl that is slightly larger than the saucepan on top.

7. Place the dark chocolate and cacao butter in the bowl and let the heat from the water melt them, about 8 to 10 minutes. Stir to make sure any chunks melt completely.

8. Mix in the liquid stevia and remove the bowl from the saucepan. Let the chocolate cool on the countertop for 10 minutes, until it thickens slightly. This will make the chocolate easy to spread without it being runny.

9. Line a rimmed baking sheet with parchment paper.

10. Slowly pour the chocolate onto the prepared baking sheet and spread it evenly with a spatula. The chocolate should be no more than ¼ inch thick. Sprinkle the matcha coconut topping evenly on top.

Approximate macros per serving: ————————
Calories: **232** • Fat: **20g** • Protein: **5g** • Net Carbs: **6g** • Fiber: **1g**

11. Place the baking sheet in the refrigerator for 30 to 45 minutes, until the chocolate is completely hardened.

12. Break the chocolate into 2- to 3-inch pieces.

No-Bake Blueberry Cheesecake Cups

SERVES 4 • **PREP TIME:** 20 minutes, plus 30 minutes chilling time
COOK TIME: —

When I was in my twenties, I made no-bake blueberry cheesecakes regularly. There's just something about that forkful of cream cheese filling with graham crackers and a blueberry compote that is simply satisfying. I never thought I would make it again after going gluten-free and then keto, but I was able to create a nutty crust that is reminiscent of the crust that I've always loved!

Cover with foil and store in the refrigerator for up to 3 days.

jenny's tip

If you can find it, swap regular cream cheese for lactose-free cream cheese.

FOR THE NUTTY CRUST:

¼ cup raw pecan halves, chopped

¼ cup sliced almonds, chopped

1 tablespoon unsalted butter, softened

2 teaspoons granulated Swerve

FOR THE CHEESECAKE FILLING:

1½ tablespoons gelatin

¼ cup warm water

1 cup heavy cream

1 (8-ounce) package cream cheese, softened

¼ cup plus 2 tablespoons granulated Swerve

1 cup fresh blueberries

1. Place the crust ingredients in a small bowl and stir to combine. Evenly distribute the mixture between four 4-ounce ramekins or mini cocottes. Gently press down on the tops with a spoon and set aside.

2. In a small bowl, dissolve the gelatin in the water. Stir and let sit for 1 minute.

3. Place the heavy cream, cream cheese, and Swerve in a stand mixer. Whip on medium speed for 30 seconds. Scrape down the sides of the bowl and whip for 20 seconds more.

4. Pour the dissolved gelatin into the bowl with the cream cheese mixture. Whip for 20 more seconds. Scrape down the sides of the bowl and whip for another 20 seconds, until fluffy.

5. Spoon the cream cheese mixture into the ramekins on top of the nutty crust. Smooth the tops. Cover and refrigerate for 30 minutes or until set. Just before serving, top the cheesecakes with the blueberries.

Approximate macros per serving:
Calories: **441** • Fat: **42g** • Protein: **7g** • Net Carbs: **12g** • Fiber: **2g**

Strawberry Mousse

SERVES 4 • **PREP TIME:** 5 minutes • **COOK TIME:** —

 Store any extra mousse in the refrigerator for up to 2 days.

Need a quick sweet treat that the entire family will enjoy? You can make this light strawberry mousse in a chilled blender in less than 5 minutes!

1 teaspoon gelatin

1 tablespoon warm water

1 cup heavy cream, cold

¼ cup fresh strawberries, chilled and chopped, plus a few extra sliced for garnish

1. Place the jar of a blender in the refrigerator to chill for an hour or up to overnight.

2. In a small bowl, dissolve the gelatin in the water. Stir and let sit for 1 minute.

3. Pour the heavy cream into the chilled blender and add the chopped strawberries. Cover and blend for 20 to 30 seconds.

4. Scrape the sides of the blender and then pour the dissolved gelatin over the strawberry mousse. Whip for another 20 seconds, until thick.

5. Transfer to small glasses and top with extra sliced strawberries.

Approximate macros per serving:
Calories: **202** • Fat: **20g** • Protein: **0g** • Net Carbs: **2g** • Fiber: **0g**

Cocoa-Dusted Almonds

SERVES 8 • **PREP TIME:** 5 minutes • **COOK TIME:** —

Transfer the almonds to a mason jar. Cover and store in the pantry at room temperature for up to 5 days.

You can serve these cocoa-dusted almonds by themselves or as part of a charcuterie board at any gathering. They're also great in a packed lunch or as an on-the-go treat.

2 teaspoons granulated Swerve

1 teaspoon coconut oil, melted

1 cup raw almonds

2 tablespoons unsweetened cocoa powder

1. Combine the Swerve and coconut oil in a medium-sized bowl and stir to mix.

2. Add the almonds to the bowl and mix with the oil.

3. Sprinkle the cocoa powder on top and toss to coat each almond well.

Approximate macros per serving: ——————
Calories: **234** • Fat: **20g** • Protein: **9g** • Net Carbs: **4g** • Fiber: **5g**

Peanut Butter Fat Bombs

SERVES 12, 1 fat bomb per serving • **PREP TIME:** 10 minutes, plus 1 hour freezing time • **COOK TIME:** 3 minutes

I keep a stash of these peanut butter fat bombs in the freezer so I can grab a piece after dinner to enjoy as my dessert or when I need a little extra fat during the day. Other types of nut butter, such as almond and cashew, are great alternatives to peanut butter. But c'mon, who doesn't love peanut butter?!

½ cup unsweetened peanut butter

¼ cup cacao butter

¼ cup ghee

1 teaspoon unsweetened cocoa powder

¼ teaspoon ground cinnamon

8 drops liquid stevia, or 1 teaspoon granulated Swerve

1. In a small saucepan, combine the peanut butter, cacao butter, and ghee. Turn the heat to medium-low and stir to melt everything together, about 3 minutes.

2. Turn off the heat, sprinkle in the unsweetened cocoa powder and cinnamon, then add the stevia and stir.

3. Pour into a 12-cavity silicone mold, then freeze for at least 1 hour.

Transfer to a zip-top freezer bag and store in the freezer for up to 1 month.

Approximate macros per serving: ——————
Calories: **452** • Fat: **44g** • Protein: **2g** • Net Carbs: **7g** • Fiber: **3g**

Coconut Butter Bites

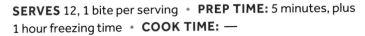

❄ *Transfer to a zip-top freezer bag and store in the freezer for up to 1 month.*

jenny's tip

Make these Coconut Butter Bites a kid-friendly treat by using a fun silicone mold like this mini Lego-man that my stepson, Diego, loves!

SERVES 12, 1 bite per serving • **PREP TIME:** 5 minutes, plus 1 hour freezing time • **COOK TIME:** —

Frozen coconut butter with a dusting of salt and hemp hearts creates a fun, fatty treat that's best enjoyed straight out of the freezer!

½ teaspoon hemp hearts

¼ teaspoon sea salt

1 cup coconut butter, melted

Sprinkle the bottom of a 12-cavity silicone mold with the hemp hearts and salt. Slowly pour the melted coconut butter into the mold and freeze for 1 hour.

Approximate macros per serving: ——————
Calories: **401** • Fat: **44g** • Protein: **0g** • Net Carbs: **0g** • Fiber: **0g**

Supercharged Nut Coffee

SERVES 1 · **PREP TIME:** 2 minutes · **COOK TIME:** —

Rise and shine; its mac nut coffee time! A cup of this drink tastes like a treat because it's so creamy that you can't even tell there's no dairy in it. Just blend, blend, blend the ingredients together in a blender until you have a creamy, frothy elixir that's guaranteed to give life after that first sip.

1½ cups hot brewed coffee

½ cup unsalted macadamia nuts

2 tablespoons collagen peptides

1 teaspoon vanilla extract

10 drops liquid stevia

½ teaspoon ground cinnamon

1. Place all the ingredients in a blender and blend on low for 10 seconds.

2. Increase the speed to medium and continue blending for 15 seconds.

3. Increase the speed to high and blend for another 15 seconds.

4. Check to make sure the consistency is smooth and creamy. Blend for a few more seconds if you still see some chunky bits.

Jenny's tips

There's no need to soak the macadamia nuts ahead of time. Just use the raw nuts straight out of the bag.

A little bit of nut pulp will sink to the bottom of your cup as you drink this coffee. To prevent that, stir between sips.

Approximate macros per serving: —————
Calories: **382** · Fat: **24g** · Protein: **32g** · Net Carbs: **16g** · Fiber: **3g**

Iced Matcha

SERVES 1 • **PREP TIME:** 3 minutes • **COOK TIME:** —

I've been hooked on matcha since I started eating keto, thanks to my friend Diane Sanfilippo. She made me a warm, creamy cup of matcha goodness during one of my visits, and I've had a cup each day ever since. I created my own version inspired by hers, and I love it iced even during wintertime!

½ cup warm water

⅓ cup coconut milk

2 scoops (30g) collagen peptides

2 teaspoons cacao butter

1 teaspoon matcha powder

10 drops liquid stevia

1 cup ice

1. Place all the ingredients except the ice in a large cup or wide-mouth jar.

2. Use an immersion blender or frother to blend everything together for 10 to 15 seconds, until well combined. You'll know it's ready when you see frothy goodness rise to the top after you turn off the blender!

3. Transfer to a drinking glass and add ice.

jenny's tip

Prepare this the night before and just add the ice for a quick grab-and-go drink to take with you.

Substitute your favorite milk for the coconut milk.

Approximate macros per serving: —————
Calories: **195** • Fat: **11g** • Protein: **20g** • Net Carbs: **6g** • Fiber: **0g**

Pink Drink

SERVES 1 • **PREP TIME:** 15 minutes • **COOK TIME:** —

The infamous "pink drink" from Starbucks has created quite a buzz among the keto community on social media as an indulgent drink of choice for those who are looking for more than just coffee. Here is my homemade version that costs less than a dollar per serving!

<table>
<tr><td>2 pomegranate tea bags</td><td>10 drops liquid stevia</td></tr>
<tr><td>1 cup warm water</td><td>¼ teaspoon vanilla extract</td></tr>
<tr><td>2 tablespoons collagen peptides</td><td>2 tablespoons heavy cream</td></tr>
</table>

1. Steep the pomegranate tea bags in the water for 5 minutes.

2. Remove the tea bags and stir in the collagen, stevia, and vanilla extract. Once the collagen dissolves, let the tea cool for 10 minutes.

3. Pour the tea in a tall glass filled with ice and stir in the heavy cream.

Jenny's tip

Use other types of berry-red tea bags in lieu of the pomegranate.

Approximate macros per serving:
Calories: **147** • Fat: **11g** • Protein: **23g** • Net Carbs: **1g** • Fiber: **0g**

Avocado and Coconut Milk

SERVES 1 • **PREP TIME:** 2 minutes • **COOK TIME:** —

During my younger days in the Philippines, my dad would top ripe avocados with powdered milk and a little sugar, and we'd eat it for dessert. Avocados are abundant there, so avocado desserts and avocado shakes are pretty popular. This quick dessert always takes me back in time whenever I make it!

1 cup ice

1 Hass avocado, peeled, pitted, and cubed

⅓ cup full-fat coconut milk

¼ cup water

8 drops liquid stevia

Place all the ingredients in a tall glass. Use a spoon to stir and mix well. The avocado chunks will break down into tinier pieces that will blend deliciously with the coconut milk.

Approximate macros per serving:
Calories: **258** • Fat: **25g** • Protein: **1g** • Net Carbs: **9g** • Fiber: **2g**

Cinnamon Hot Cocoa

SERVES 1 • **PREP TIME:** 2 minutes • **COOK TIME:** —

Cozy up with a soft blanket and a cup of this rich, homemade hot cocoa that will warm you from within!

⅓ cup full-fat coconut milk

⅓ cup hot water

1 tablespoon unsweetened cocoa powder

2 teaspoons cacao butter

8 drops liquid stevia, or 1 teaspoon granulated Swerve

Pinch of ground cinnamon, for garnish

Pour the coconut milk in a large heatproof cup or mug and microwave it on high for 1 minute. Transfer the milk to a high-speed blender and add the rest of the ingredients. Blend for 30 seconds until frothy. Pour the mixture back into the mug and sprinkle the cinnamon on top.

Approximate macros per serving:
Calories: **305** • Fat: **31g** • Protein: **1g** • Net Carbs: **9g** • Fiber: **2g**

Citrus Electrolyte Drink

SERVES 6 • **PREP TIME:** 5 minutes, plus 1 hour to chill
COOK TIME: —

During my first week on keto, I felt sluggish because of electrolyte imbalance, so I added a little salt to my water. I wanted something refreshing to sip throughout the day, so I jazzed up my usual spa water and transformed it into this citrus electrolyte drink!

6 cups water

1 lemon, sliced

1 lime, sliced

3 fresh mint sprigs

1 teaspoon sea salt

Place all the ingredients in a glass pitcher. Pour in the water and mix to dissolve the salt. Refrigerate for 1 hour to chill and infuse the water with the citrusy flavors.

jenny's tip

You can reuse the pitcher with the leftover citrus 2 or 3 times. Just refill the pitcher with water, replace the mint sprigs with new ones, and add another teaspoon of salt to make another batch.

Approximate macros per serving: —————
Calories: **5** • Fat: **0g** • Protein: **0g** • Net Carbs: **1g** • Fiber: **0g**

Berry Keto Smoothie

SERVES 1 • **PREP TIME:** 2 minutes • **COOK TIME:** —

Nut butter, berries, and your choice of milk whipped up with coconut oil and collagen create this creamy and satisfying drink that will help you feel energized without the sugar high.

¾ cup nut milk of choice

½ cup fresh strawberries

½ cup fresh blueberries

2 scoops collagen peptides

2 tablespoons almond butter

1 tablespoon coconut oil, melted

1 cup ice

Place all the ingredients in a high-speed blender. Blend for 15 to 20 seconds, until frothy. Pour into a glass before serving.

Approximate macros per serving:
Calories: **436** • Fat: **34g** • Protein: **13g** • Net Carbs: **16g** • Fiber: **7g**

ACKNOWLEDGMENTS

To all my readers, followers, and Cook and Savor community who tune in and hang out with me every week on Instagram for meal prep Sundays—thank you for all your feedback and advice and for sharing my passion for good food and great music. It warms my heart to see you cook my recipes to enjoy with your families.

To my friends and coworkers who continually inspire me and bravely accepted the challenge to be my recipe testers—high five to each one of you!

To Diane—mad props to you for helping me brainstorm ideas for this book, for being so generous in sharing your knowledge, and for always believing in me.

To my editors, Pam, Holly, and Charlotte—thank you for providing me feedback early on and for helping me fine-tune each chapter. I know this is a unique book, and I appreciate all your efforts.

To my publisher, Erich, and the rest of the Victory Belt team—thank you for the opportunity to share my meal prep strategy and techniques that have helped me and my community of meal preppers these past few years.

Last but not the least, to my husband, Will, my forever sidekick in the kitchen who fearlessly wore many hats to help me make this book happen. My sous chef, hand model, dishwasher, recipe tester, critic, and camera man. You are the best partner I could ever ask for.

RECOMMENDED PRODUCTS, BRANDS, AND RESOURCES

Here are the products, brands, and resources that I recommend.

You can shop these items here: **easyketomealprep.com/resources**

Pantry Items

 365 Coconut Milk
wholefoods.com

 Jade Leaf Ceremonial Matcha
jadeleafmatcha.com

 Balanced Bites Meals
balancedbites.com

 Balanced Bites Spices
balancedbites.com

 Big Tree Farms Coconut Aminos
bigtreefarms.com

 Bob's Red Mill (unsweetened shredded coconut, almond flour, coconut flour)
bobsredmill.com

 Fourth and Heart Ghee
fourthandheart.com

 Epic Pork Rinds
epicprovisions.com

 Kasandrinos Olive Oil
kasandrinos.com

 Miracle Shirataki Noodles
miraclenoodle.com

 Primal Kitchen (avocado oil, avocado oil spray, mayonnaise)
primalkitchen.com

 Primal Palate Spices
primalpalate.com

 Red Boat Fish Sauce
redboatfishsauce.com

 SweetLeaf Liquid Stevia
sweetleaf.com

 Swerve Sugar Replacement
swervesweet.com

 Vital Proteins Collagen Peptides
vitalproteins.com

Quality Protein Sources

 Five Marys Farms
fivemarysfarms.com

 Vital Farms
vitalfarms.com

 Moink Meats
moinkbox.com

Storage Containers and Cooking Equipment

 All-Clad Skillets and Saucepans
all-clad.com

 Instant Pot
instantpot.com

 Ball Mason Jars
masonjars.com

 Staub Cast Iron Pans
staub-online.com

 Blenders
omegajuicers.com
vitamix.com

 Zwilling Knives
(9-inch chef's knife, 7-inch santoku, and 7-inch nakiri)
zwilling.com

 Cuisinart Food Processor – 9 cup
cuisinart.com

 Glass Containers
glasslockusa.com
pyrexhome.com

Books

 Keto Quick Start
by Diane Sanfilippo

 Made Whole
by Christina Curp

 The Keto Diet
by Leanne Vogel

 Craveable Keto
by Kyndra Holley

ALLERGEN INDEX

RECIPE	PAGE	⊘	⊘	⊘
Easy Peasy Hard-Boiled Eggs	52	✓		✓
Italian Casserole	54			✓
Will's Favorite Beef Tapa	56	✓	✓	✓
Chimichurri Pork Chops	58	✓	✓	✓
Sheet Pan Beef and Veggie Kabobs	60	✓	✓	✓
Everything Baked Chicken	62			✓
Weeknight Bolognese	64	✓	✓	✓
Blistered Green Beans	66		✓	✓
Spaghetti Squash Noodles	68	✓	✓	✓
Sheet Pan Veggies	70	✓	✓	✓
Chimichurri	72	✓	✓	✓
Goat Cheese and Salmon Spread	73		✓	✓
Spiced Vinegar	74	✓	✓	✓
5-Ingredient Everything Seasoning	75	✓	✓	✓
Loaded Hamburger Hash	90		✓	✓
Savory Breakfast Plate	92	✓	✓	✓
Turkey Mushroom Sauté	94	✓	✓	✓
Crispy Carnitas	96	✓	✓	✓
Pesto Meatballs	98		✓	✓
Carne Asada	100	✓	✓	✓
Chicken Adobo	102	✓	✓	✓
Blanched Bok Choy	104	✓	✓	✓
Zesty Slaw	106	✓	✓	✓
Balsamic Roasted Tomatoes	108	✓	✓	✓
Turmeric Garlic Cauliflower Rice	110	✓	✓	✓
Roasted Sweet Peppers and Onions	112	✓	✓	✓
Zucchini Noodles	114	✓	✓	✓
Chili Oil	116	✓	✓	✓
Pico de Gallo	118	✓	✓	✓
Shortcut Shakshuka	134	✓		✓
Sheet Pan Cauliflower Fried Rice	136	✓		✓
Filipino Turbo Chicken	138	✓	✓	✓
Wonton Noodle Soup	140	✓	✓	✓
Cheeseburger Casserole	142			✓
Baked Salmon	144	✓	✓	✓
Instant Pot Roast	146	✓	✓	✓
Mediterranean Couscous	148		✓	✓
Nutty Tahini Broccoli	150	✓	✓	✓
Three-Veggie Chop Suey	152	✓	✓	✓
Shredded Kale and Pepita Pecan Salad	154	✓	✓	
Jalapeño Cauliflower Mash	156	✓	✓	✓
Pan-Roasted Garlic Oil	158	✓	✓	✓
Olive Gremolata	160	✓	✓	✓
Steak Rub	162	✓	✓	✓
Blender Pancakes	178			
Loaded Breakfast Frittata	180			✓
Five-Spice Meatballs	182	✓		✓
Chicken Korma	184	✓	✓	✓
Instant Pot Beef Barbacoa	186	✓	✓	✓
Easiest Lasagna	188			✓
Black Pepper Chicken	190	✓	✓	✓

RECIPE	PAGE	⃠	⃠	⃠
Shrimp Fried Rice	192	✓	✓	✓
Lo Mein	194	✓	✓	✓
Classic Veggie Fajitas	196	✓	✓	✓
Garlic Naan	198	✓	✓	✓
Oven-Baked Bacon	200	✓	✓	✓
Tomato Avocado Salad	202	✓	✓	✓
Tangy Onion and Jalapeño Relish	204	✓	✓	✓
Aji Verde Sauce	206	✓		✓
Chili Garlic Paste	208	✓	✓	✓
Ghee	210	✓	✓	✓
Mayonnaise	212	✓		✓
Instant Pot Eggs en Cocotte	222	✓		✓
Ginger Chicken	224	✓	✓	✓
Kung Pao Chicken	226	✓	✓	
Coconut Macadamia–Crusted Pork Chops	228	✓	✓	
Juicy Pan-Fried Chicken Tenders	230	✓	✓	✓
Asian Glazed Halibut	232	✓	✓	✓
Sheet Pan Smoky Shrimp	234	✓	✓	✓
Instant Pot Salsa Chicken	236	✓	✓	✓
Basil Slaw	238	✓		✓
Ginger Scallion Sauce	240	✓	✓	✓
Giardiniera	242	✓	✓	✓
10-Spice Seasoning	244	✓	✓	✓
Seed Crackers	248	✓	✓	✓
Parmesan Crisps Three Ways	250		✓	✓
Pepperoni Pizza Bites	252		✓	✓
Packable Cheese Board	254			
Crudité Platter with Herbed Dip	256		✓	✓
Deviled Eggs	258	✓		✓
Guacamole and Pork Rinds	260	✓	✓	✓
Spiced Nut Mix	262	✓	✓	
Instant Pot Chicken Wings	264	✓	✓	
Garlic Parmesan Chicken Wings	266		✓	✓
Italian Roll-Ups	268		✓	✓
Pork Rind Nachos	270		✓	✓
Peanut Butter Cookies	272	✓		
Nutty Chia Pudding	274	✓	✓	
Chocolate Bark	276	✓	✓	
No-Bake Blueberry Cheesecake Cups	278		✓	
Strawberry Mousse	280		✓	✓
Cocoa-Dusted Almonds	282	✓	✓	
Peanut Butter Fat Bombs	284	✓	✓	
Coconut Butter Bites	286	✓	✓	✓
Supercharged Nut Coffee	288	✓	✓	
Iced Matcha	290	✓	✓	✓
Pink Drink	292		✓	✓
Avocado and Coconut Milk	294	✓	✓	✓
Cinnamon Hot Cocoa	296	✓	✓	✓
Citrus Electrolyte Drink	298	✓	✓	✓
Berry Keto Smoothie	300	✓	✓	

GENERAL INDEX